The Agonist

Volume XI, Issue II, Spring 2018

The Persisting Enigma of Nietzsche's Zarathustra

Nicholas Birns   Richard J. Elliott   Christopher England

Rainer J. Hanshe   Lawrence J. Hatab   Dirk R. Johnson

Kevin LaGrandeur   Jeffrey Lucas   Alec Ontiveros

Thaís Helena Smilgys   Alessio Tommasoli

Nietzsche Circle, Ltd.
Editor-in-Chief
Yunus Tuncel

Editors	**Managing Editor**	**Book Review Editors**
Kaity Creasy	Alec Ontiveros	Kaity Creasy
Luke Trusso		Richard J. Elliott
		Jack Fitzgerald
		Joshua Hall

Editors (for German)	**Proofreaders**
Sabine Roehr	Jack Fitzgerald
Michael Steinmann	Joshua Hall

Advisory Board

Lawrence J. Hatab	David Kilpatrick	Vanessa Lemm
Dirk R. Johnston	Jeffrey Malpas	Paul van Tongeren
Kimerer LaMothe	Graham Parkes	James Luchte

Graphic Design	**Electronic Publisher**
Seth Binsted	Hasan Yildiz and Alec Ontiveros

Interns
Lauryn-Ashley Vandyke

Advertising Donations
Donations can be made at http://www.nietzschecircle.com

Nietzsche Circle and The Agonist Website Design and Maintenance
Hasan Yildiz

Letters to the editors are welcome and should be emailed to:
nceditors@nietzschecircle.com.
The Agonist is published twice a year by Nietzsche Circle, Ltd. P.O. Box 575,
New York, NY 10113, U.S.A.

Website: http://agonist.nietzschecircle.com/wp/
For advertising inquiries, email Lauryn-Ashley Vandyke at
vandykelaurynashley@gmail.com.

Contents

Book Reviews

Editors' Introduction

"But when he peered about himself and searched for the comforters of his solitude, oddly enough, it was cows huddled together on a knoll; their nearness and smell had warmed his heart" – Thus Spoke Zarathustra

Welcome to the new issue of The Agonist! *Thus Spoke Zarathustra* is many different things to different readers: proto-modernist manifesto, convoluted prose-poem, Nietzsche's failed attempt at a novel, a parody of scripture, a revisionist Socratic dialogue, recitation of the eternal return, etc. Historically speaking, it is perhaps best remembered as announcing the end of humanism, with Zarathustra prophesizing the coming of the enigmatic "overhuman." Nietzsche certainly thought it was his masterpiece, and never tired of singing its praises. As he proclaimed triumphantly in *Ecce Homo*: "Among my writings my Zarathustra stands by itself. With this book I have given mankind the greatest gift it has ever been given." It would seem like hyperbole if not for the thousands of pages of ink spilled since its publication. Perhaps most confounding, is that while Nietzsche's radical intellectual challenges to moral and cultural values may have been too early for the late nineteenth century, we may be too late. Like all of his mature works, the text invites a multitude of interpretations, and we have included what we hope to be several fresh contributions to the conversation.

We would like to thank all of our contributing writers, the members of our new advisory board, the editorial staff of at *The Agonist*, and of course our readers. We look forward to hearing from you along with suggestions for any future topics.

The Editorial Board
April 2018

We begin with a brief thought experiment by managing editor Alec Ontiveros:

A Sage Approaches
A Creative Reinterpretation of *The Madman,* [125] *GS.*

Alec Ontiveros

[342]

A Sage Approaches☐There I see it happening in the dark moonlight, just now as the sun begins to rise again from its valley, a sage solemnly walks into the town. Few remain awake—except for the thief and the jester commiserating with each other beneath the old clock tower—that garrulous relic of the golden age, built proud with its byzantine facade that only seemed to obscure its labyrinthine interior—that cold truth that time is bottomless and thus it is in all ways unbecoming. From the shadow of this truth emerges the sage, asking peacefully, "What is time? Do you know what is time?" As the jester did not long to know the hour any longer, for time is only confusion, it was confusion that wrang out, "Perhaps it is just past midnight, for I somehow feel the urge to do this all over again." Through a sieve of reason, the thief aptly rhymes, "Morning sun, if midnight is past felt, the day is now dealt, your first conscious memory, will be time's soliloquy, it is One." Gleeful by the easiness of having believed a transvaluation occurred, the sage rests calmly next to the companions.

"Why have you emerged from the night, do you not know that god is dead?" the jester cries out, unsettled by the cold brought by the sage's arrival. "There are no morning sacraments for you to declare, all that is left to till from the earth is that which falls off, unrooted in its accelerating spin, for with no god any longer the earth is not fixed to itself, for nothing holds it back from accelerating to its end, for we have nothing left to confirm, you and your wisdom, perhaps, arrived too late," the thief promptly chants. "Too late? I thought you said that time is One!" reflected the sage. "One?" the thief said, no longer hiding behind the guise of stolen phrases. For which the pride of the jester so gallantly emerged, "I have heard this statement before, that time is One, I have heard it so many different ways that I almost forgot what it means, the 'new' historicists used to say before the moment arrived when god was killed, the wise and the pious all agreed, that there was only one time, but now we know that to be an illocutionary fable, you surely have arrived far too late!"

Immediately the statement vanished within itself for at that moment the clock bellowed as it called again the bells of midnight, and with it the thief and the jester began to kneel before the sage, for they too far strung from the daylight had forgotten about this old facsimile of humanity's ancient error, to think that time owes itself to revision as passively as the rooster will soon not crow in the yet still dusk. And before their prostrations and adorations, the sage began to laugh, "No, get up you wandering souls, I choose not to become a conduit for time, for time is rotten and beset to decay! Time is rotten because it fulfilled its purpose at the beginning yet it still lives, thus life is the evaporation caused by its bottomless gravity. It lives not but is for its own conclusion! It always was but never is until it finally will be! So it has been thus becomes so it never will be! All is obscured by its massive void of nothingness, for when it was so it is, so it always will be. Ever fleeing away from the fixity of itself. How too this illusion gripped us with madness, it taught us to see a zero as a circle rather than as a spiraling staircase, and thus we thought everywhere we could build this sense of our confusion, this part of us that would one day become our understanding. Yet we did not realize how in doing so, we would lead all back to nothing, for rather it is from nothingness that comes everything, thus all is included in the nothing. Yet no thing is not the thing that is its thing-itself, for itself is its thing that is not yet no thing."

Here the sage fell silent as the thief begins to etch a counterfeit rhyme, "Fiction, rhythm, holy rhyme, god's corpse is rotten, and thus so is time." "How you have stolen the music from my heart, but what you have played for me is all of the dissonance the harmony transcends. For time is not rotten for nothing after all, it is rotten because it is withering away as from it emerges the exuberance of all things fixed that become eternal." The sage exits the market square humming an ancient tune, as an old lamppost perched in a tenebrous shadow shakes with life and the festival begins again.

Essays

What Kind of Text is *Zarathustra*?
Reflections on Art and Philosophy, Appearance and Truth in Nietzsche's Writings

Lawrence J. Hatab

In *Thus Spoke Zarathustra* II: "On the Poets," Zarathustra identifies himself as a poet (*Dichter*) and yet claims that he has become weary of poets because they "lie too much" and are too superficial in not thinking deeply enough. *Zarathustra* is itself a poetic text that is saturated with philosophical concepts. The passage on poets seems to disturb the import of aesthetic elements in *Zarathustra*, which is surprising since the language of the text can be distinguished from its deeper artistic force, given Nietzsche's remark that "the whole of *Zarathustra* can be considered music" (*EH* "Books: Z" 1). Why are poets (and poetry) superficial, and what is the meaning of lying *too much*? What bearing does this have on Nietzsche's claim in the *Genealogy* that art runs counter to the ascetic ideal because it sanctifies lying (*GM* III: 25)? How are poetry and concepts or music and language related in *Zarathustra*? These questions touch on central issues in Nietzsche's writings having to do with art and philosophy, language and thinking, truth and lies.

Poetry and Lying

In *Z* II: "On the Scholars," Zarathustra says he has abandoned that mode of intellectual work. The next section is "On the Poets," where Zarathustra claims that all thoughts of permanence are only a parable (*Gleichnis*), a term that appears often in *Zarathustra* and in this section is connected with poetry. Zarathustra declares that he is a poet but also that "poets lie too much," and they lie because they "know (*wissen*) too little."[1] Parables embody poetic lies

---

[1] The notion of poets lying too much is first mentioned earlier in *Z* II: "Isles of the Blest." In this article I employ the following translations: *BGE*, *BT*, and *EH* are by Walter Kaufmann in *Basic Writings of Nietzsche* (New York: Random House, 1966). *D* is by R.J. Hollingdale in *Daybreak* (Cambridge University Press, 1982). *GM* is by Carole Diethe in *On the Genealogy of Morality* (Cambridge University Press, 2007). *TL* is from *Writings From the Early Notebooks*, eds. Raymond Geuss and Alexander Nehamas (Cambridge University Press, 2009), pp. 253-264. *TI* is by Walter Kaufmann in *The*

and deception, in that they tell of "gods and *Übermenschen*." Zarathustra declares that he is weary of all this; in Part III he will even say he is ashamed of being a poet (Z III: "Tablets" 2). The section "On the Poets" is striking because poetic language in *Zarathustra* and other texts is often praised as an alternative to traditional knowledge claims, and *Gleichnis* is frequently deployed in a positive manner in *Zarathustra*.[2] But here knowledge seems to be a corrective for poetry and parables (even of *Übermenschen*!)—more precisely for *too much* deception, which is not a rejection of poetry outright. Zarathustra goes on to say that poets old and new are superficial and shallow, that "they have not taken their thought deep enough" (*Sie dachten nicht genug in die Tiefe*). Their beautiful creations must pale before something ugly, which is spelled out in the next two sections of the text.

In "On Great Events," something momentous looms ahead. The next section, "The Soothsayer," foretells the nihilistic effects of eternal recurrence: that everything is in vain because of endless repetition. Zarathustra is stricken by this and has a terrible dream where he sinks into life-denial. But images of children and laughter presage the next section, "On Redemption," where the eternal recurrence of life is affirmed, which redeems what has been by willing its return—a "vision" that composes (*dichten*) the past, present, and future into a unified necessity. This composition is contrasted with life-denying, vengeful "fable-songs (*Fabelliedern*) of madness." The vision will become a direct experience of eternal recurrence in Part III ("On the Vision and the Riddle"); and the thought of eternal recurrence will be counter-posed to Zarathustra's admission of shame at being a poet (Z III: "Tablets" 2).

What is evident in the span of texts I have sketched is an ambiguous set of juxtapositions—poetry, knowledge, experience, a confrontation with nihilism, and composition of the life-affirming thought of eternal recurrence—the upshot of which is not easy to fathom. In addition, the seeming critique of poetic deception does not sit well with an important moment in a later text, *GM* III: 25, where Nietzsche declares that the life-denying ascetic ideal is not countered by science (because of its belief in truth) but by art, because in art "*lying* sanctifies itself and the *will to deception* has good conscience on its side." What are we to make of all this? We seem to face a tangled intersection of truth, lying, thought, and poetry, which I will attempt to sort out in what follows.

Portable Nietzsche (New York: Viking Press, 1954). Z is by Graham Parkes in *Thus Spoke Zarathustra* (Oxford University Press, 2005). I have occasionally altered the translations.
[2] Some examples: *Z* I: "Gift-giving Virtue," *Z* II: "Isles of the Blest," *Z* II: "Grave Song," and *Z* III: "Homecoming."

The Question of Truth

Nietzsche's writings issue a complicated posture on the question of truth.[3] Contrary to some readings (and some of his own rhetoric), I believe that he accepts and employs certain motifs of truth, as long as they are purged of metaphysical foundationalism and restricted to a more modest, pluralized, and contingent perspectivism. Even if knowledge is variable, historical, and born out of human interests, that does not render it false, arbitrary, or uncritical (*GS* 2, 191, 209, 307). In a notebook entry, Nietzsche says that when *the* truth is put aside, particular truths can still be worth fighting for (*KSA* 7: 19 [106]). There are also provocative moments when Nietzsche hints at a pluralized "objectivity," wherein the more perspectives one can adopt, the more adequate one's view of the world will be: "The *more* affects we allow to speak about one thing, the *more* eyes, different eyes, we can use to observe one thing, the more complete will our 'concept' of this thing, our 'objectivity' be" (*GM* III: 12).[4] In a notebook passage, this kind of perspectival aggregation fits the task of "*seeing things as they are*" (*KSA* 9: 11 [65]).

I will organize the discussion of truth around the following distinctions, which I denote as T1, T2, and T3: (T1) Throughout his writings Nietzsche affirms a negative, tragic truth of becoming, in the sense that flux must be recognized as a primal force that renders all forms and structures ultimately groundless.[5] Various passages speak of a difficult, fearsome truth that must be faced to counter a myopic fixation on life-enhancing beliefs.[6] (T2) Because of Nietzsche's commitment to the tragic truth of becoming, positive doctrines of truth that presuppose foundational conditions of "being" are denied and often designated as "appearances" or "errors."[7] Although such structures are life-enhancing, they must still be unmasked as a "falsification" of experience (*BGE* 24). (T3) Despite the ammunition becoming provides for Nietzsche's charge that traditional truth conditions are appearances or errors, he does notice the trap in sustaining the binary discourse of reality-appearance and truth-error. Falsification is the flip-side of verification. Undermining "truth" also

---

[3] For an excellent overview and analysis of the question of truth in Nietzsche, see R. Lanier Anderson, "Nietzsche on Truth, Illusion, and Redemption," *European Journal of Philosophy* 13:2 (2005), 185-225.

[4] See also *BGE* 211.

[5] See *BT* 21-22; *TI* "Reason" 2 and 6; *KSA* 13: 11 [72].

[6] See *BGE* 39; *GM* I: 1; *GS* 110. In this way, Nietzsche is exploring a negative truth that so far has been forbidden (*EH* P: 3).

[7] *TL*, *GS* 354-355, *TI* "Errors," *EH* "Books: Z" 8, *KSA* 12: 2 [108] and 13: 11[72].

destabilizes any designation of "error," because error can only be measured by some governing truth standard: "The true world—we have abolished. What world has remained? The apparent (*scheinbare*) one perhaps? But no! *With the true world we have also abolished the apparent one*" (*TI* "True World" 6). What are we left with, then? I believe there is a positive sense of "apparent truth" (T3) in Nietzsche's thought that strikes a balance between the negative truth of becoming (T1) and the error of being (T2), a balancing act that especially fits the perspective of art.

The Question of Appearance[8]

In *The Birth of Tragedy* Nietzsche's account of the Dionysian and the Apollonian deployed a reality-appearance distinction apparently in line with that of Kant and Schopenhauer. Yet Nietzsche came to recognize the misleading way in which he used the term "appearance" (*Schein, Erscheinung*) in *BT*, namely in a seeming metaphysical sense contrasted with an underlying "reality" (thus as "mere" appearance).[9] In an 1888 note Nietzsche denies that a metaphysical reality-appearance binary was operating in *BT*: "truth" there is tragic nihilation and disintegration (T1); the will to appearance is a life-saving formation of meaning for the Greeks, an artistic "lie" that is *more primal* and *more profound* than the will to truth.[10]

A central theme in Nietzsche's philosophy is that traditional forms of knowledge run up against the limit of radical becoming, and that such forms arise from the "fixing" effects of language and grammar. For instance, the flux of phenomena is converted into a series of discrete "facts" because we are misled by the individuated spacing of words (*WS* 11).[11] Yet Nietzsche often insists that such "errors" are necessary for human functioning and survival.

---

[8] Throughout his writings, Nietzsche employs different words that can be translated as "appearance" (e.g., *Schein, Erscheinung, Scheinbarkeit*). There does not seem to be a sustained technical distinction between these words in Nietzsche's usage. Whether the meaning is appearance, mere appearance, illusion, deception, etc., can only be discerned in context.

[9] In his "Attempt at Self-Criticism" (1886), Nietzsche rejected the use of Kantian and Schopenhauerian terminology because he was all along attempting "new valuations" that were utterly at odds with the philosophies of Kant and Schopenhauer (*BT* ASC: 6). For an account of the difference between *BT* and Schopenhauerian metaphysics, see Béatrice Han-Pile, "Nietzsche's Metaphysics in *The Birth of Tragedy*," *European Journal of Philosophy* 14/3 (2006), 373-403. See also James I. Porter, *The Invention of Dionysus: An Essay on* The Birth of Tragedy (Stanford, CA: Stanford University Press, 2000), 57-77.

[10] *KSA* 13: 11 [415] and 17 [3].

[11] See also *BGE* 34 and *TI* "Reason" 5.

Indeed, identifying these errors is not on that account an objection (*BGE* 4). In *BGE* 268, Nietzsche calls the communicating character of words "the most powerful of all powers" because of its life-serving value. Even further, in a notebook passage, after outlining the prejudices of language, Nietzsche adds: "we think *only* in the form of language. . . . we cease to think when we refuse to do so under the constraint of language." An 1887 note states that the linguistic order of thinking is "a scheme that we cannot throw off" (*KSA* 12: 5 [22]). A comparable claim is given in a published work: "we have at any moment only the thought for which we have the words at hand" (*D* 257). Remarks such as these make it hard to read the "falsification" of experience as fitting any familiar sense of falsehood if one cannot even *think* outside of such errors, and especially if the fluid excess of becoming cannot really count as a "measure" for any kind of discernible truth.

As indicated earlier, once the traditional binary of reality and appearance is rejected, it does not make sense to talk of "mere" appearance in a deficient sense. The idea of appearance can be given a positive sense of temporal emergence and showing forth ("She appeared from behind the curtain"), which can fit some of Nietzsche's usage of the term. Indeed, two notebook entries describe appearance as a non-metaphysical *reality*, which makes possible the constructed forms of meaning that, while ultimately groundless, are necessary for life.

> "Appearance" itself belongs to reality (*Realität*): it is a form of its being; . . . Appearance is an arranged and simplified world, at which our *practical* instincts have been at work; for *us* it is perfectly real (*recht*); that is to say, we live, we are able to live in it: *proof* of its truth for *us*. . . . the world, apart from our condition of living in it . . . does *not* exist as a world "in itself," it is essentially a world of relations: possibly it has a different aspect from every point: its being (*Sein*) is essentially otherwise (*anders*) from every point. (*KSA* 13: 14 [93])

> The world of "phenomena" is the adapted world that we *perceive to be real*. . . . The antithesis of this phenomenal world is *not* "the true world," but the formless unformulable world of the chaos of sensations—thus *another kind* of phenomenal world, one "unknowable" for us. (*KSA* 12: 9 [106])

Here Nietzsche posits *two* levels of phenomena or appearance: the primal, formless flux of becoming, and the subsequent gathering of this flux into livable forms. Since *both* are designated as appearance, there is no other "reality" against which either one could be called "apparent" in a deficient sense. Indeed, what the tradition had called the (merely) apparent world is for Nietzsche "the only world" (*TI* "Reason" 2); the traditional distinction between the apparent world and the true world is in fact a distinction between the actual world and *nothing* (*KSA* 13: 14 [184]). At times Nietzsche exchanges the true-false binary for *degrees* of appearance (*BGE* 230, *KSA* 12: 9 [40]), that is to say, *how* apparent something is to us. In *GS* 54, Nietzsche decisively rejects the distinction between appearance and some opposite "essence" or "thing in itself." And here Nietzsche identifies *his* understanding of appearance with "that which lives and acts effectively." So, appearance—*in life*—is not *mere* appearance, because it names real (living) events that nonetheless cannot satisfy traditional standards of metaphysical realism or dogmatic certainty. An 1881 notebook passage pointedly captures Nietzsche's positive appropriation of appearance: "My philosophy is an *inverted Platonism*: The further something is from true being, the more clear, beautiful, and better it is. Living in appearance (*Schein*) is the goal" (*KSA* 7: 7 [156]).

What bearing can all this have on coming to terms with Nietzsche's charge of "falsehood" that we are examining? An 1881 *Nachlass* passage (*KSA* 9: 11 [156]) might help. There Nietzsche distinguishes between three degrees of "error" in relation to an eternal flux: "the crude error of the species, the subtler error of the individual, and the subtlest error of the creative moment (*Augenblick*)." Species-form is the crudest error because it corrals differences into a common universal. The assertion of the individual is a "more refined error" that comes later, rebelling against commonality in favor of unique forms. But then the individual learns that it itself is constantly changing and that "in the smallest twinkling of the eye (*im kleinsten Augenblick*) it is something other than it is in the next [moment]." The creative moment, "the *infinitely small moment* is the higher reality and truth, a lightning image out of the eternal flow." The "higher reality and truth" of the creative moment is thus an "error" in a quite different sense compared to the species-error and the individual-error.

Even the notorious fragment "On Truth and Lie in an Extra-Moral Sense"—the supposed source of Nietzsche's critique of truth as an erroneous superimposition of stable form onto a stream of flux—shows some leeway in distinguishing creative formation from secured form. The metaphorical transfer of fluid and variable experience to fixed words and concepts is actually preceded by the more original operation of "intuited metaphors" and "images" that are closer to the flux of experience by being singular, unique apprehensions; and such pre-conceptual apprehension is associated with an artistic imagination that does not fall into the trap of fixed words and concepts (*TL*, 256-58).

Nietzsche often articulates the meaning of appearance in terms of creativity and art. In an 1887 note he claims that truth is not "found" in reality, it is *created* as a manifestation of will to power (*KSA* 12: 9 [91]). In *GS* 58, Nietzsche insists that "knowledge" of "things" has its origin in historical moments of creativity bequeathed to us by innovative thinkers. Such creations are called *appearances*; yet with familiarity over time, such appearances harden into supposed "essences"— only to be replaced by new creations in the course of history. In his writings Nietzsche quite naturally associates the idea of creative appearance with art (*BT* ASC: 5); he even calls art "the *good* will to appearance" (*GS* 107). Since art had traditionally been excluded from the realm of strict truth, Nietzsche is happy to trade on the idea of "fiction" to goad a metaphysical faith by celebrating art as "deception" (*GS* 344). Yet we should be circumspect in considering such talk of deception replacing truth, because Nietzsche thinks that "artistic deception" is the creative characteristic of "everything that is" in nature and the mark of reality and truth (*KSA* 13: 11 [415]). Indeed, an early notebook entry offers that "art forms are more real (*realer*) than reality (*Wirklichkeit*)," and that the latter is an imitation of the former (*KSA* 7: 9 [133]).

All told, it seems that the tragic truth of becoming (T1) renders *any* thought formation groundless, and thus a (life-enhancing) "deception" in the light of *that* truth: "*We have need of lies* in order to conquer this reality, this 'truth,' that is, in order to *live* . . . . man must be a liar by nature, he must above all be an *artist*. And he *is* one: metaphysics, religion, morality, science—all of them only products of his will to art, to lie, to flight from 'truth, to *negation* of 'truth.'" (*KSA* 13: 11 [415]).[12] The critique of traditional thought systems amounts to this: they themselves are (artistic) creations with no ultimate foundation, yet they interpret themselves otherwise—they claim to be *true* and nothing like "art." For Nietzsche, art has a special status because it does not pretend to be grounded in truth; art is thus more *truthfully* deceptive. An 1873 note among drafts for *TL* puts the point dramatically: "Art treats appearance (*Schein*) *as* appearance, therefore it does *not* want to deceive, *it is true*" (*KSA* 7: 29 [17]).[13] The deceptive character of art, therefore, is far from falsehood in the strict sense; it "accords" with tragic truth. Art is a lie in the familiar sense of a *knowing* falsehood, a deliberate departure from standard notions of truth. The tradition lies while

---

[12] This note was written in 1888. References such as this from the later period and the overall discussion I am advancing challenge the assumption of Maudemarie Clark (and others) that Nietzsche abandoned his early anti-truth talk in favor of a more scientific orientation.

[13] See also *GS*, 1886 Preface: 4. There Nietzsche praises the Greeks for their love of appearances: they were "superficial—*out of profundity*." The last phrase is *aus Tiefe*, and so this remark clashes with the charge that poets are superficial in *lacking* depth or profundity.

thinking it is telling the truth, perhaps like pathological liars who come to believe their lies.[14]

Here is a summation thus far in terms of my three distinctions concerning truth. In the light of tragic truth (T1), *all* formations of thought are deceptive lies. When thought presumes to be a foundational construction of truth (T2), it can be called deceptive from a *critical* standpoint, as a "violation" of tragic truth. Art has no pretense of being foundational and so its mode of deception can have a positive sense (T3). Indeed, *all* formations of thought can have a positive meaning if taken in a more modest way as perspectival "creations" that are limited by tragic truth. T2 assumes truths that are incompatible with T1, and thus "false." T3 does not and need not fit the perfect sense of what T2 assumes; yet as life-enhancing and workable within perspectival possibilities, T3 can be "true" in a limited manner, but at the same time "false" from the standpoint of its *literal* sense—so that, for instance, the notion of a discrete "thing" is not literally true (measured against T1), but it is functionally and pragmatically *apt*. T3 does not commit the error of metaphysical truth (T2). Borrowing from an artistic sense, T3 can be "fictional" compared to literal accuracy, but useful and disclosive in its own way.[15] Artistic fiction works in its own way too, but *admits* its fictional nature, thus being more "true" to T1. Art's *overt* non-foundational posture gives it a distinctive position among cultural productions, and that is why Nietzsche uses the metaphor of art to characterize all forms of thought.

Falsehood in Greek Poetry

To round out this discussion, I offer some remarks about ancient Greek poetry that may help us better comprehend Nietzsche's account of appearance and falsehood.[16] The Greeks were well aware from the earliest times that poetic performances depicted something different from "actual" events. Traveling bards would enthrall audiences with emotionally and musically charged tales about gods and heroes—culturally significant events embellished with heightened language for maximum effect. And such performances were a "pause" set aside from normal life pursuits. What interests us is that a word commonly used to denote this "difference" was *pseudos*, usually translated as

---

[14] In an episode of the *Seinfeld* program, George is trying to teach Jerry how to beat a lie detector. He says: "If you believe it, it's not a lie." We now have a President who seems to be a serial liar.

[15] See Justin Remhof, "Scientific Fictionalism and the Problem of Inconsistency in Nietzsche," *Journal of Nietzsche Studies* 47/2 (Summer 2016), 238-246.

[16] What follows is drawn from my *Nietzsche's* On the Genealogy of Morality: *An Introduction* (Cambridge University Press, 2008), 184-86.

"false." Yet the context of this use and the cultural status of poetry would undermine the idea that *pseudos* here meant "falsehood" as the sheer opposite of truth.[17] Indeed, *pseudos* was a word with remarkable flexibility, the various senses of which could only be discerned in different contexts of use. Unlike our language, the Greeks used this same word to denote an "error" and a "lie," that is, a mistaken statement and an intentional falsehood.

The common attribution of "falsehood" to poetry extends the ambiguity of *pseudos* even further. First of all, given the *competitive* nature of Greek poetry, individual poets would use *pseudos* to target other poets—in this context "false" would mean "inferior" or "ineffective" or "not *my* poetry." More importantly, *pseudos* could refer to what we would call "fiction" as opposed to "fact," yet not in the binary sense that we might expect. The Greek word usually translated as "fact" is *ergon*, which had a general meaning of something *done* rather than something merely *said*—a distinction that could apply to the "different" sphere of poetic speech. The poetic sense of *pseudos* would be closer to what we would call verisimilitude, or "fictive truth." In the Greek sense, fictive truth would not only refer to the way in which poetic language could "resemble" reality, but also to its persuasive power to enthrall the audience and absorb it in the *reality* of the poetic fiction (eliciting wonder, joy, fear, etc.). This is precisely one meaning of the Greek word *mimēsis*—not merely representational likeness, but the psychological *identification* of an audience with a poetic performance (more on this shortly). Nietzsche recognized this mimetic power of poetic "appearances" in *The Birth of Tragedy*. Greek drama only enhanced mimetic power because it went beyond a bard's mere narration in speech to actors embodying poetic speech in action. The word *drama* in Greek meant something *done*, and so Greek theater showed a *conjunction* of "fiction" and "fact," saying and doing, in the Greek sense. In any case, Nietzsche recognized the world-disclosive effects of mimetic poetry in tragedy. He says that poetic images were not "symbolic" because they possessed a living capacity to create their own world (*BT* 8); here dramatic "fiction" was not a departure from reality because it staged powerful scenes of "a world with the same reality and irreducibility that Olympus and its inhabitants possessed for the believing Hellene" (*BT* 7).

If we keep in mind the cultural status of poetry in the Greek world, then their attributions of *pseudos* to poetry (even in pre-philosophical periods) cannot be construed as castigations or even diminishments of poetic language—but rather, among other things, as a gesture to the "different" sphere of poetry

---

[17] The following remarks are drawn from Louise H. Pratt, *Lying and Poetry from Homer to Pindar* (Ann Arbor, Michigan: University of Michigan Press, 1993), Ch. 1.

together with its revelatory power. Poetry could not simply be an entertaining diversion for the Greeks (akin to our enjoying works of fantasy), because poetry carried world-disclosive and life-guiding significance. Even the notion of "fictive truth," therefore, might not suffice for capturing the ambiguities surrounding the Greek sense of poetic *pseudos*.

One final historical note on the ambiguity of poetic falsehood: Some texts tell of the commingling of *pseudos* and truth (*alētheia*) in poetic speech. The *Odyssey* is marked by many alternations between deceptive and true accounts (sometimes mixed together) in the manner of verisimilitude and other senses (see 8. 487ff. and 19. 203). In Hesiod's *Theogony*, the muses (who inspire poetry) are said to be capable of both verisimilitude and straightforward truth: "We know how to say many false things (*pseudea*) that are like (*homoia*) true sayings (*legein etumoisin*); but we also know, when we want to, how to speak true things (*alēthea gēurusasthai*)" (23-28). In epic poetry, *homoia* did not connote deceptive resemblance but equivalence in some aspect.[18] My overall point is that Nietzsche the classical philologist must have been aware of the many complex senses in which Greek texts depicted poetry, falsehood, and truth. This might help us better understand the evident ambiguities in Nietzsche's own deployment of falsehood-language in his celebration of art.

The Limits of Poetic Deception

Having covered the meaning and importance of artistic "deception" in Nietzsche's thought, we must return to the question of what Zarathustra meant by claiming that poets lie too much. I believe the answer is to be found in (1) the high status of conceptual thinking in *Zarathustra* and other writings; and (2) the experiential impact of the thought of eternal recurrence, which engenders a dark tragic *truth* (T1) and the task of affirming life in the face of that truth. To begin, in *BT* Nietzsche tells us that the *meaning* of tragic myth was not directly expressed in the "word drama" of poetry, and that his own conceptual efforts are initiating such an understanding: "the structure of the scenes and the visual images reveal a deeper wisdom than the poet himself can put into words and concepts" (*BT* 17). It seems evident that tragic poetry by itself would not suffice for Nietzsche's intellectual task. Philosophical concept formation (e.g., "the tragic") provides a deepened and enhanced comprehension of the meaning of pre-reflective cultural phenomena. Indeed Nietzsche maintains that the

---

[18] See Bruce A. Heiden, "The Muses' Uncanny Lies, Theogony 27 and Its Translators," *American Journal of Philology* 128/2 (Summer 2007), 153-175.

emergence of theoretical reason and science in the Greek world was not the elimination of aesthetic, creative forces, but their modification (*BT* 15); again, all forms of thought can be called artistic creations.

Nietzsche here announces something that continues to resonate in his writings: philosophical understanding is crucial, but with concept formation it has to distance itself from preconceptual, artistic cultural forms. Such distance harbors the danger of philosophical alienation from, even hostility toward, preconceptual culture. The advent of philosophy in the Greek world is the original case study. Presocratic philosophy in many ways was reflective of tragic meanings (see *PTAG*). But with Socrates and Plato philosophy became antagonistic toward tragic poetry. Concept formation resisted the force of becoming to create structures of "being" (T2) that could quell or govern flux for the purpose of secured knowledge and conscious mastery of life. But Nietzsche maintains that here philosophy suppressed its *own* creative, and thus *artistic* character (T3).

In *The Birth of Tragedy*, Nietzsche aims for much more than a historical analysis of Greek culture; he is meditating on the very nature of philosophy and its future prospects, indeed the coming of a new tragic age (*EH* "Books: *BT*" 4). Philosophy must always draw on preconceptual sources, namely pre-existing artistic productions and philosophy's own creative impulses that cannot be reduced to its conceptual products. Platonic philosophy and its descendants represent an antagonistic, eliminative disposition toward preconceptual/poetic/tragic origins. In *BT*, Nietzsche poses the question of whether this antagonism between philosophy and the tragic world-view is inevitable and beyond resolution (*BT* 17). He thinks not, and suggests an image for reconciliation in the figure of an "artistic Socrates" (*BT* 14, 15, 17), a thinker who is not averse to aesthetic modes, who indeed can employ such modes in the practice of philosophy. One naturally thinks of the deliberate deployment of literary and artistic devices in the course of Nietzsche's philosophical writings. In any case the importance of art in Nietzsche's thinking cannot be restricted to art forms per se; what he calls a "higher concept of art" is embodied in the artist-philosopher (*KSA* 12: 2 [66]).

It is not enough, however, to coordinate conceptual and artistic production in philosophy. Such coordination implies a tragic limit because of the indigenous abyss at the heart of philosophy (indeed all cultural production) owing to its creative, rather than foundational, base. Reflecting back on *The Birth of Tragedy*, Nietzsche claims that in this work he had discovered the *concept* of the tragic, that he sees himself as "the first *tragic philosopher*," the first to offer a "transposition of the Dionysian into a philosophical pathos" (*EH* "Books: *BT*"

3).[19] At the same time, tragic philosophy is here called the "antipode" to a pessimistic philosophy because it says Yes to becoming in all its constructive-destructive energies; it embraces "the eternal joy of becoming," and its "Dionysian philosophy" entails the "teaching (*Lehre*) of 'eternal recurrence,' that is, of the unconditional and infinitely repeated circular course of all things."

The thought (*Gedanke*) of eternal recurrence is the basic concept (*Grundconception*) of *Zarathustra* (EH "Books: *Z*" 1); its comprehensive entailment of all life is obviously a philosophical notion rather than a poetic image. Poetry has the edge over *traditional* philosophy in being overtly creative, non-foundational, and life-like in its imagery. And the narrative character of *Zarathustra* makes the text as such poetic. But poetry cannot suffice for the philosophical impulse to think holistically and to comprehend the deepest of questions: Can natural life on its own terms be meaningful and affirmable? The thought of eternal recurrence forces us to confront this question by ruling out any alternative to immediate life—even the alternative of nothingness.[20]

We might sort out the questions posed in this essay by attending to the *Ecce Homo* Preface and the section "Books: *Z*." Nietzsche calls himself a "disciple of the philosopher Dionysus" (P 2)—thus sustaining the tragic philosophy first announced in *BT*. Philosophy as Nietzsche understands it entails the *courage* to face the truth (P 3)—the tragic truth of becoming named in T1. Eternal recurrence precludes any hopes for salvation or a better life; it requires the demolition of all old ideals ("Books: *Z*" 8)—thus in line with T1. The traditional posit of a "true world" is a *lie* (T2) as measured by T1. Nietzsche describes his *Zarathustra* as the "greatest gift" to humanity because of its profound reach into tragic truth (P 4); and its poetic character can fit T3 because it can coexist with tragic truth in being an *overt* "lie," in forming an image-world that does not pretend to be a foundational truth.

It is at this point that we might orchestrate the poetic and philosophical elements in *Zarathustra*. In *Ecce Homo*, Nietzsche specifically stresses the poetic character of the text, indeed by way of the word *Gleichnis*. He describes how *Zarathustra* "came to" him, came over him in an inspired state, with an involuntary eruption of image (*Bild*) and *Gleichnis*. In such a state, "you ride on every *Gleichnis* to every truth" ("Books: *Z*" 2). The text is called a Dionysian deed that "creates truth" (in the poetic sense); it represents the greatest force of

---

[19] Nietzsche cites Heraclitus as a possible exception to his claim of originality.

[20] See my *Nietzsche's Life Sentence: Coming to Terms With Eternal Recurrence* (New York: Routledge, 2005), 85-89.

Gleichnis, the "return of language to the nature of imagery (*Bildlichkeit*)" ("Books: *Z*" 6). This sounds like a retrieval of preconceptual language as noted in *BT*. But then in this same section of *EH*, Nietzsche describes the figure of Zarathustra as expressing the concept (*Begriff*) of the Dionysian, as one who has thought (*Gedacht*) the most abysmal thought (*Gedanken*)—eternal recurrence—in an affirmative posture (see also "Books: *Z*" 1).

We can say that the entire text of *Zarathustra* is poetic, an artistic "lie" in a positive sense. But poetry is not the full story; it lies "too much" if it holds off philosophical thinking, which can comprehend the tragic truth about life in the deepest and most comprehensive manner, and then come to terms with this truth—not just in thought or art but in *life*, in one's existential comportment. Poetry may be insufficient for philosophical understanding, but *no* text can stand in for the *task* announced in *Zarathustra*. Yet such an extra-textual task is not utterly divorced from the intra-textual and sub-textual forces in Nietzsche's narrative.

Music and Dance

The existential task presented in *Zarathustra* concerns the affirmation of natural life, especially its visceral embodiment, passionate drives, and instinctive energies—which were precisely the targets of spiritualized or rationalized philosophies and their conceptions of truth (T2). The philosophical register of *Zarathustra* can never be separated from its poetic character, which liberates the text from prevailing truth standards. But the modern understanding of poetry is generally restricted to language arts and written texts. Ancient Greek poetry was orally sung in live performances, and tragic poetry added enactment along with musical accompaniment and dance.[21] Music and dance enact sub-textual, embodied elements of language (tempo, rhythm, tone, gesture), which *communicate* with visceral life-energies that cognitive/verbal emphases suppress or conceal.

The text of *Zarathustra* has scores of references to, and enactments of, song, singing, and dance. And in *Ecce Homo* we read: "Perhaps the whole of *Zarathustra* can be considered music—certainly a rebirth in the art of *hearing* was one of its preconditions" (*EH* "Books: *Z*" 1). Dance is surely the epitome of (musical) embodiment, and it is given a high status in *Zarathustra*: "Only in the dance can I tell the parable (*Gleichnis*) of the highest things" (*Z* II: "Grave Song"). Nietzsche

---

[21] Nietzsche's early text on Greek music drama emphasized our misunderstanding of tragic poetry because of the modern separation of poetry from music. See *The Greek Music Drama*, trans. Paul Bishop (New York: Contra Mundum Press, 2013).

depicts Zarathustra as a dancer who affirms life in the face of eternal recurrence (*EH* "Books: *Z*" 6). In *GS* 84, Nietzsche implicates dance in the historical origin of poetry, and in *Zarathustra* dance seems to be a relief from Zarathustra being ashamed of poetry (*Z* III: "Tablets" 2). In *TI* "Germans" 7, Nietzsche says: "thinking wants to be learned like dancing, as a *type* of dancing. . . . A *noble* education has to include *dancing* in every form, being able to dance with your feet, with concepts, with words; do I still have to say that you need to be able to do it with a pen too—that you need to learn to *write*?"

As indicated above, dance is the clearest indication of embodiment, and its connection with poetry and music can help illuminate "sub-verbal" elements in language that communicate in a non-cognitive manner by way of tempo, rhythm, tone, gesture, and artistic effects (see *EH* "Books" 4). Such elements reflect precisely those natural energies in life to which the text of *Zarathustra* points. But a focus on music and dance pushes beyond modern "textual" notions of poetry to "sub-textual" effects that can be traced back to the historical emergence of language out of human embodiment. Such sub-linguistic origins are addressed in Nietzsche's discussions of language in relation to gesture and music.

Language, Gesture, and Music

In *HH* 216, Nietzsche claims that language originated in gestures and facial expressions, together with the automatic, immediate imitation of these phenomena in face to face experience, which is natural in adults as well as children (called "motor mimicry" in modern psychology). Such was a direct communication of shared meanings (such as pleasure and pain). From such common comprehension, Nietzsche says, a "symbolism" of gestures could arise, with verbal sounds first coupled with the gestures, and then after familiarity operable by way of the sound symbols alone. We can understand the sense of this in how much gestures and facial expressions play an important role in face to face speech.[22]

Nietzsche occasionally discusses what can be called mimetic psychology, especially in his reflections on Greek art. An early essay, "Greek Music Drama," mentions the audience's sympathetic identification with the sufferings of tragic heroes. [23] And *The Birth of Tragedy* contains several relevant treatments. Apollonian and Dionysian forces are exhibited in nature herself, *before* the

---

[22] For research that confirms Nietzsche's account, see David McNeill, *Gesture and Thought* (The University of Chicago Press, 2005), especially Ch. 8.
[23] *The Greek Music Drama*, 32.

mediation of artistic works (*BT* 2). Forming and deforming powers are intrinsic to nature's course, and dreams and intoxicated states (both of which exceed conscious control) are preconditions for the more cultivated manifestation of Apollonian and Dionysian powers, particularly those of language and music. Artists are said to "imitate" primal natural energies, which could not mean representational simulation, but rather the more performative sense of "impersonating" these energies in artistic practices (impersonation being one of the meanings of *mimēsis* in Greek). Indeed, nature itself urges expression in bodily gestures and movements (*BT* 21). Singing and dancing then exhibit an enchanted, ecstatic elevation, a quasi-divine transformation where one is not really an artist because one "has become a work of art" (*BT* 1).

In many respects, Nietzsche associates the Dionysian with music (*BT* 6, 17), especially its immediate emotional force that "overwhelms" conscious individuation. The Apollonian is associated with poetic language and theatrical technologies that shape a more individuated world. But since music and language are coordinated in tragic drama (*BT* 21), immediate disclosive force still operates in its performances. As indicated earlier, poetic metaphors are not "symbolic," they possess a living power to disclose a world (*BT* 8). Tragic drama produced a Dionysian effect of mimetic identification, originally embodied in choral impersonation, where one acts "as if one had actually entered into another body, another character" (*BT* 8). An early note on tragic drama reads: "All art demands a 'being outside oneself,' an *ekstasis*; it is from here that we take a step to the drama, by *not* returning within ourselves, but entering into an unfamiliar being, in our *ekstasis*, as if bewitched" (*KSA* 7: 2 [25]).

In general terms Nietzsche considers music to be equiprimordial with gesture as a foundation for language, particularly in terms of how a speaker's *tone* accompanies gesture symbolism. Rhythm and pitch intonations, according to Nietzsche, provide a common field of comprehension that renders the communicative power of language possible. [24] This is one reason why the Dionysian was essential for Greek tragedy in Nietzsche's eyes, because the "universal" element behind Apollonian language could be presented through the

---

[24] See the 1871 fragment "On Music and Words," found translated (by Walter Kaufmann) in Carl Dahlhaus, *Between Romanticism and Modernism*, trans. Mary Whittall (Berkeley: University of California Press, 1980). In "The Dionysiac World View," gesture and tone are originally instinctive, without consciousness, but not without purpose. See *The Birth of Tragedy and Other Writings*, eds. Raymond Geuss and Ronald Spiers (Cambridge University Press, 1999), 134. An 1871 note offers tone as the universal foundation of language, with differences in gesture generating different forms of language (*KSA* 7: 12 [1]).

combination of music, gesture, and dancing that embodied the poetic performance (*BT* 6).[25] Nietzsche thought that the Greeks had a capacity largely lost in modern experience, namely a "third ear" that could hear the musical background of language (*BGE* 8). We could say that Nietzsche's answer to the question of how language could express something beyond its arbitrary phonic forms (given the differences in words across different languages) would not be in terms of universal cognitive conditions, but universal corporeal conditions of gesture and musicality. And his reasons for restricting language to a certain "fictional" status would follow from our tendency to separate distinct words from 1) the flux of experience and 2) the embodied forces behind verbal speech. Yet it seems that the first tendency is the more apt target because the corporeality of language in gesture and tone is said by Nietzsche to make language possible and it is not hard to intimate its indigenous function in embodied speech.

Nietzsche's many remarks about style in writing have a bearing on this discussion. He calls good style the communication of internal effects through the enactment of signs, tempo, rhythm, tone, and gesture (*EH* "Books" 4). An 1882 letter offers a "doctrine of style," proclaiming that writing must have life and affect, approximate poetic rhythm, and perform "gestures" (*Gebärde*) through "length and brevity of sentences, punctuation, the choice of words, pauses, the sequence of arguments."[26] Tempo plays a central role in texts (*BGE* 28), along with tone and rhythm, all of which harkens back to ancient modes of style that were grounded in oral speech and the practice of reading texts aloud, even reading aloud to oneself, something lost when we read only with our eyes (*BGE* 247). In *WS* 110, Nietzsche points to what is missing in written language, "the modes of expression available only to the speaker: that is to say, gestures, emphases, tones of voice, glances." Yet one can still intimate the sonic dynamics of language if one reads with a "third ear" (*BGE* 246).

Nietzsche's approach to style surely connects with his estimation of music as a primal force communicating life energies and passions, which was central to performances of Greek tragedy. It was Socratic dialectic that drove "music out of tragedy under the lash of its syllogisms" (*BT* 14). Ideas became lifeless because philosophers had "wax in their ears," making them unable to listen to embodied life, since "life is music" (*GS* 372). Even Nietzsche's critique of the

---

[25] See Kathleen Higgens, "Nietzsche on Music," *Journal of the History of Ideas* 47/4 (Winter 1986), 663-672.
[26] Letter to Lou Salomé, cited and discussed by Tracy Strong, "In Defense of Rhetoric: Or How Hard It Is to Take a Writer Seriously: The Case of Nietzsche." *Political Theory* 41/4 (August 2013), 507-532.

tradition has a sonic, musical dimension. The subtitle of *TI* is "How One Philosophizes with a Hammer." The Preface emphasizes "sounding out" idols, with a hammer that acts as a "tuning fork."[27]

This last section of my essay can help flesh out what Nietzsche meant by identifying *Zarathustra* with music. In structure, style, and effects, the text can be seen as tapping into and eliciting life energies with sub-textual intimations. At the same time, all the elements covered in this essay aim to show that *Zarathustra* is an indissoluble blend of poetry, philosophy, music and language, such that none of the elements by themselves could suffice for the kind of thinking Nietzsche advances in the text. Yet I think a tilt toward philosophy is called for. We should not overestimate the importance of art in *Zarathustra* or underestimate its philosophical character. "Too much art" would diminish Nietzsche's evident interest in stimulating comprehensive thought and its effect on real life.

---

[27] Nietzsche's writings have been examined in the light of music and musical structure. See for example: Michael Gillepsie, "Nietzsche's Musical Politics," in *Nietzsche's New Seas*, eds. Michael Gillepsie and Tracy Strong (University of Chicago Press, 1988), 117-149; Bruce Ellis Benson, "Nietzsche's Musical Askesis for Resisting Decadence," *Journal of Nietzsche Studies* 34 (Autumn 2007), 28-46; and Babette Babich, "*Mousikē Technē*: The Philosophical Practice of Music in Plato, Nietzsche, and Heidegger," in *Between Philosophy and Poetry: Writing, Rhythm, History*, eds. Massimo Verdiccio and Robert Burch (New York: Continuum, 2002), 171-180. The musical character of Nietzsche's texts goes beyond structural matters because reading his work can be like listening to music. See Tracy Strong, Introduction to *Twilight of the Idols*, trans. Richard Polt (Indianapolis, IN: Hackett. 1997), vii-xxviii. Yet here structural questions can still obtain, in that a text can be read in a manner that is not restricted to linear, logical structure, so that the text as a whole can gather and unify dissonant themes and conflicting elements, which can be read as contrapuntal rather than contradictory. See Babette Babich, "On Nietzsche's Concinnity: An Analysis of Style," *Nietzsche Studien* 19 (1990), 59-90.

Dionysian Logos:

On Nietzsche's Poetic Typology and the "Closing Melodies" of *The Gay Science*, *Zarathustra*, and *Beyond Good and Evil*

Rainer J. Hanshe

As the Eiffel Tower, arch symbol of modernity, rose to completion in Paris in 1889, Nietzsche collapsed in the Carlo Alberto Piazza in Torino, not far from the Mole Antonelliana, a newly constructed synagogue that, perhaps fittingly, became in the late 20th century Italy's National Museum of Cinema. Constructed between 1863 and 1889—thus spanning Nietzsche's entire adult life—the Antonelliana was one of the philosopher's most beloved architectural structures and, "because of its absolute drive for elevation," he said it reminded him "of nothing so much as my *Zarathustra*. I have baptized the tower Ecce Homo, and in spirit have opened an enormous free space around it."[1] Thus, a synagogue evokes for Nietzsche not only his greatest gift to mankind, but is sanctified by him with the name of his exalted autobiography. The significance of architecture for Nietzsche is crystallized in this account, which illustrates both his view that buildings must be conducive to thinking, and that grand style itself is a form of architecture, revealing his concern with structure and design—as will be illustrated, and the musical sense of the following term is meant deliberately to convey a fitting and pertinent resonance, this is evident in the very *composition* of his books.

Two days prior to his collapse, Nietzsche corrected the proofs of the *Dionysus Dithyrambs*, which would be his penultimate book, then added this dedication: "Sing to me a new song: The world is transfigured and all the heavens are glad."[2] Signing it "The Crucified One," the parodist of world history offered us his last gift, not the tender of redemption, but a final series of Pindaric-inspired songs. If his first published book was not a poetic work as he later thought it should have been—a point endlessly reiterated but perhaps here of particular and more precise relevance—his last book was: he *did* dare say

---

[1] KSB 8: 566. From a letter dated December 30, 1888.
[2] KSB 8: 575. This sentence is taken from a postcard Nietzsche wrote to Heinrich Köselitz.

what he had to say as a poet, but as a different kind of poet altogether. Aside from his two strictly poetic works, the *Idylls of Messina* and the *Dionysus Dithyrambs*,[3] what is illustrated by his juvenilia, the poems that accompany the first edition of *Human, All Too Human*, both editions of *The Gay Science*, and *Beyond Good and Evil* as well as *Thus Spoke Zarathustra*, which Nietzsche himself referred to as "a poem and not a collection of aphorisms" (KGB III, 1[373]), is that the Dionysian-inflected Socratic satyr wrote poetry almost continually from the age of nine till his collapse at 44. Considering his critique of the poet, which may be even more stringent than Plato's,[4] how do we account for Nietzsche's continuing engagement with poetry? Is there, as most critics believe, actually a disparity or contradiction here that cannot be resolved?[5] From his early work

---

[3] The *Idylls of Messina* and the *Dionysos Dithyrambs* were the sole works of Nietzsche's composed strictly of verse. The first, a cycle of eight poems, was featured in a magazine edited by his publisher Schmeitzner in 1882 and thereafter listed by Nietzsche himself on the back cover of his subsequent books as one of his works. The latter was his last complete work. During his final sane days, he was proofreading the book.

[4] Phillip Pothen expresses this same view: "Nietzsche's suspicion concerning art is perhaps the greatest of any since Plato's, and even, it might be said, *including* Plato's." See Pothen's *Nietzsche and the Fate of Art* (London: Ashgate, 2002), 12.

[5] Even if there is a contradiction, Nietzsche radically challenges the notion of contradiction and problematizes it in his philosophy, but this still has not been sufficiently considered. One key passage regarding this can give a brief sense of how contradiction must be vigorously rethought when considering his philosophy: "Immense is the ladder on which he [Zarathustra] climbs up and down; he has seen further, willed further, *achieved* further than any man. He contradicts with every word, this most affirmative of all spirits; in him *all opposites are fused together into a new unity*" (EH: "Zarathustra" §6, emphasis added). See also, to give just a few pointed examples, D §1, GS §297, and most famously, Z: III.2 §2, where the eternities of the future and the past, two stringently opposed or contradictory things, *fuse together*, just as Nietzsche fuses together the opposing 'forces' of dark and light in the concluding poem of BGE, "Aftersong: On High Mountains." In addition, since Nietzsche frequently reconceived and changed his views, theoretically, it is misguided to demand or expect that there be an overarching consistency to his oeuvre. But this forces us to ask, what specifically does contradiction signify in Nietzsche's work? How do we interpret it? For two explorations of contradiction in Nietzsche's thought, see Wolfgang Müller-Lauter, *Nietzsche: His Philosophy of Contradictions and the Contradictions of His Philosophy* (Illinois: University of Illinois Press, 1999), and Walter H. Sokel, "On the Dionysian in Nietzsche: Monism and its Consequences," *New Literary History*, Vol. 36, No. 4 (Autumn 2005): 501–520. For a slightly different and expanded version of the latter essay, see the archive essay section of the Nietzsche Circle website. For Sokel, to note one basic aspect of his essay, the seemingly contradictory positions espoused in Nietzsche's work are actually an enactment of *justice*, of Nietzsche's thinking out

through to his final writings, I believe that Nietzsche actually sustains a distinction between two poetic types, and it is always as the second type that he writes when he poetizes, though he is even in an *agon* with poetry when writing prose. "It is noteworthy," Nietzsche professes, "that the great masters of prose have almost always been poets, too—if not publicly then at least secretly, in the 'closet.' Good prose is written only face to face with poetry. For it is an uninterrupted, well-mannered war with poetry: all of its attractions depend on the way in which poetry is continually avoided and contradicted" (GS §92).[6] If this reveals how, even in avoiding it, prose can be deeply informed by poetry and that one may remain a poet even when not writing verse, let us proceed to the two poetic types as conceived by Nietzsche to elucidate his intensified Platonic polemic, and to clarify why, in fact, there is no irresolvable disparity.

The first type, which is generally if not always the subject of Nietzsche's critique whenever he speaks of the poet and of poets, is a nihilist who uses language to lie and enchant. In promulgating universal ideals, this type maintains views that are false, untenable, and possibly dangerous, for the universal homogenizes what is particular, distinct, and resolutely singular. Such humanistic ideals are essentialist and elide social, cultural, and epochal differences in claiming to represent what is fundamentally human and particular to all, whereas Nietzsche complicates the "human," which to him is an undetermined animal whose status is ambiguous. This type of poet is first characterized in *Human, All Too Human* as one whom either escapes from the sufferings of its present age, or evades them through "coloring" them with past insights instead of developing insights particular to its own epoch.[7] In this way,

---

positions from various perspectives and giving weight to alternative views, which is emblematic of his very conception of philosophy. The following passage from Schlegel is relevant, too: "Humanity has correctly sensed that it is its eternal, necessary character to unify in itself the indissoluble contradictions, the incomprehensible enigma that emerges out of the joining together of what is eternally opposed." See Friedrich Schlegel, *On the Study of Greek Poetry* (New York: SUNY Press, 2001), 25.

[6] Mexican poet Octavio Paz made a similar observation when stating that "Language, by its own inclination, tends to be rhythm. As if they were obeying a mysterious law of gravity, words return to poetry spontaneously. At the heart of all prose, more or less attenuated by the demands of discourse, circulates the invisible rhythmic current." See Octavio Paz, *The Bow and the Lyre* (New York: McGraw Hill, 1973), 56–57. This passage is in the chapter "Verse and Prose."

[7] In BT, Nietzsche speaks of the epic and the lyric poet and Socrates as emblematic of the anti-poetic (strictly logical) stance Nietzsche opposes in philosophy and life, but those types are particular to ancient Greek poetry and different from the ones here in question.

such poets are myopic and atavistic for they sustain dying and dead religions and cultures, they are fervent acolytes, mediocre imitators as opposed to productive parodists, and they are deceptive because the sustaining comforts they claim to offer are but provisional and fleeting, thus a kind of stupefying narcotic. More serious, they render our passions inoperative and neutralize our active forces, thereby hindering us from the necessary task of continual self-overcoming (HH §148). As idealists and valets of morality, instead of instigating our necessary self-overcoming, they promote the interest of the species and faith in life as opposed to sacrificing themselves to the earth in order to create beyond themselves and serve as models of transfiguration. They are ethical teachers who, in preaching of the purpose of existence, fail to see life as an experiment, just as they fail to recognize the role contingency plays in it. But "life" needs not our faith, nor does it need to be preserved, as if we even had the power to preserve something of which we are merely a speck of dust within it.[8] "There is no denying that in the long run," Nietzsche avows, "every one of these great teachers of a purpose was vanquished by laughter, reason, and nature: the short tragedy always gave way again and returned into the eternal comedy of existence . . ." (GS §1).[9] Such ethical teachers are akin to the famous "liars" spoken of in *Zarathustra*, those who lack sufficient critical faculties and believe not only in the majority and its wisdom, but that Nature itself speaks to or is in love with and whispers secrets to them (Z: II.17). Here we have one of the supreme anthropomorphic delusions; a dose of Darwin would do such poets well. In opposition, Nietzsche's ideal is "those who do not want to preserve themselves" (Z: III.12).

In opposition to this type is the visionary poet who devotes his or her poetic power to "signposting the future" (AOM §99). Also first described in *Human, All Too Human*, this poet is one who has the imaginative capacity to create "fair images of man" [*schönen Menschenbilde fortdichten*] and does not withdraw from this

---

[8] This calls to mind Nietzsche's critique of the Stoics and their desire to live according to nature: "And supposing your imperative 'live according to nature' meant at bottom as much as 'live according to life' — how could you *not* do that? Why make a principle of what you yourselves are and must be?" (BGE §9)

[9] And is that not the ultimate height that Nietzsche wants to reach? Consider the epigraph to the third book of Z: "Who among you can laugh and be uplifted at the same time? Whoever climbs the highest mountains laughs about all tragic plays and tragic wakes." Perhaps this is too terrifying for most humans. Is not the comedian of the ascetic ideal, is not Hanswurst, the *figura* par excellence? Is not he the comic poet, or, *Zarathustra*?

world, but envisions the possibility of "great and beautiful souls,"[10] makes them visible, sustains them, and forges new models which, through exciting our envy and desire to emulate them,[11] compel us to create or engineer the future. Conceptually, this is reminiscent of Zarathustra and the *Übermensch* and is quite possibly an early instance of the burgeoning of those figures. Importantly, the poems of this type of poet are "secluded and secured against the fire and breath of the *passions*," free of delusions, decadence, "mocking laughter and gnashing of teeth, and everything tragic and comic in the old customary sense" (AOM §99), all negative qualities that Nietzsche would later employ to characterize the figure of the Sorcerer in *Also sprach Zarathustra*. In contrast, the future minded poet is capable of overcoming the spirit of heaviness and of blending knowledge and art into a new unity, clearly a further continuation of the optics of art and science Nietzsche espouses in the *Birth of Tragedy*. Such a poet is capable of creating the "golden ground" out of which "the actual *painting*—that of the ever increasing elevation of man," is constituted, and it is fitting here to think of the Mole Antonelliana and the intimate relation between architecture and style. The conceptual parallel with the *Übermensch* and Nietzsche's task of continual self-overcoming is readily apparent, too. As a poet of the future, such a type depicts only "reality" (a more scientific versus idealistic—i.e., *artistic* in what would be a negative sense for Nietzsche—view of the world) and completely ignores "all those fantastic, superstitious, half-mendacious, faded subjects upon which earlier poets demonstrated their powers. Only reality," Nietzsche emphasizes, "but by no means every reality!—he will depict a select reality!" (AOM §114) With this concluding remark, the philosopher-poet illustrates that the artistic type as he configures it is not concerned with a solely factual or historical, let alone totalizing Hegelian record of reality, but with its transfiguration. Thus, although he demands art be informed by science, and mindfully embody Enlightenment principles, its role is not exclusively scientific, let alone ruled by rationality or logic. It is also strongly guided by the faculty of the imagination.

---

[10] See BGE §12 for Nietzsche's view on how a way remains open for "new versions and refinements of the soul-hypothesis; and such conceptions as 'mortal soul,' and 'soul' as subjective multiplicity, and 'soul as social structure of the drives and affects,' want henceforth to have citizens' rights in science."

[11] Envy not in its Christian, but in its ancient Greek sense, which for Nietzsche is eminently positive: "Envy spurs men to activity: not to the activity of fights of annihilation but to the activity of fights which are contests. [...] Every great Hellene hands on the torch of the contest; every great virtue kindles a new greatness. [...] Every talent must unfold itself in fighting: that is the command of Hellenic popular pedagogy" (HC).

If many pathways to the "poetry of the future" begin with Goethe as Nietzsche pronounces (AOM §99), the poet of *Faust* is also the recipient of an incisive critique. In contradistinction to Herr Goethe, the muse of the visionary poet is not "the Eternal Feminine," but reality itself. In not recognizing that Dionysian art evolved out of the orgy, according to Nietzsche, Goethe and his dutiful acolyte Winckelmann did not understand the Greeks (TI: Ancients §4). In celebrating the Eternal Feminine, Goethe idealizes woman as such, thereby establishing a prototype that is illusory and romantic. And "when a poet is not *in love with* reality," then, Nietzsche believes, the muse only bears him "him hollow-eyed and fragile-limbed children" (AOM §135), which is perhaps to say, works of art that are indicative of a blindness toward the world (refusing for instance to recognize the role of death in life, if not in the actual creation of life,[12] to countenance the role cruelty plays in life, etc.) and completely lacking in power or mobility. In *Daybreak*, Nietzsche envisions the new poet as one who, as an arbiter of the future, must be a *seer* of the *possible* who lets "us feel in advance something of the *virtues of the future!*" And if this poet envisages virtues that will never exist on earth, they are not otherworldly virtues for "they could exist somewhere in the universe — of purple-glowing galaxies and whole Milky Ways of beauty!" Nietzsche exults. "Astronomers of the ideal, where are you?" (D §551) As Zarathustra proclaims, "But let will to truth mean this to you, that everything be transformed into what is—humanly thinkable—humanly visible—perceptible!" (Z: II.2) And that Zarathustra is precisely this kind of future minded poet is evident not only when he declares that, while he is "of today and former times," he contains something "that is of tomorrow and the day after tomorrow and times to come" (Z: II.17). His being such a poet is also apparent in his self-critical way of poetizing, for he understands the role of rhetoric and the ways in which language can be deceptive. It is apparent too in his signposting the future and transfiguring existence as well as in his willingness to sacrifice himself as opposed to longing to eternally preserve himself. His teaching is not prescriptive but suggestive, marked for instance in his announcement, "May your will say: *Let* the Overhuman be the sense of the earth!" (Z: P §3) He does not proclaim that the Overhuman is the sense of the earth, but proposes that we assign such a sense to the earth. Nietzsche always

---

[12] See Jean Claude Ameisen's eminently fascinating book, *La Sculpture du vivant. Le suicide cellulaire ou la mort créatrice* (Paris: Seuil, 2003).

speaks of created senses or meanings,[13] not ontological or metaphysical ones, such as those poets and prophets believe they hear, hence the total lack of necessity for proving the eternal return true.[14] Fundamentally, what is distinct about this type is that it *creates* truth and is a *world-governing* spirit and a destiny, all things that, Nietzsche claims, even a poet as superior as Dante fails to accomplish (EH: "Zarathustra" §6).

Importantly, it is not the world that Nietzsche ever seeks to redeem, for that would be to Christianize it and to suffer from the ideals of the first type of poet. It is only the past that he struggles to redeem, yet it is not from sin that it is to be redeemed; instead, one is *released* from the binds of temporality.[15] "I taught them all *my* composing and striving: to compose and carry into one whatever about the human is fragment and riddle and cruel-coincidence— —as poet, unriddler, and redeemer of coincidence I taught them to work creatively on the future, and creatively to redeem—all that *was*" (Z: III.12 §4). And the culmination of the latter type of poet is elaborated on when in the final section of *Twilight of the Idols* Nietzsche speaks of the *tragic* poet as one who does not

---

[13] Although Nietzsche believes that life has no inherent meaning, and there are passages in the *Nachlaβ* that concern the ability to live without meaning, he nonetheless recognizes the necessity of its role in our existence. However, as opposed to fixed or permanent meanings, such as those established metaphysically, Nietzsche implores us to recognize that all meanings are anthropomorphic, myths that we ourselves forge. And Zarathustra implies that there is a necessity for endowing one's life with *Sinne* (meaning, or sense) when he says, "And verily, if there were no sense [*Sinne*] to life, and I had to choose nonsense, this would be for me too the most choiceworthy nonsense" (Z: I.2).

[14] In a letter to Overbeck, Nietzsche notes that it is *belief* in the eternal return that gives the concept its real force, not whether it is factually accurate: "*If it is true*, or rather: if it is believed to be true — then *everything* changes and spins around, and *all* previous values are devalued" (10.3.1884). See Karl Löwith, *Nietzsche's Philosophy of Eternal Return* (California: University of California Press, 1997), 87. Having to prove the truth of the eternal return would be entirely at odds with Nietzsche's fundamental philosophical positions, for it would be to demand ontological proof where none can be had, and where such proofs are refuted. As Nietzsche says of Christianity, and following the aphorism that announced the death of God this has a different impact, an impact Danto's way of reading Nietzsche — haphazardly, in any order — would not, what is now decisive against Christianity "is our taste, no longer our reasons" (GS §132).

[15] For an elaboration of Nietzsche's notion of release, which he pits over and against redemption, see Rainer J. Hanshe, "Invisibly Revolving— —Inaudibly Revolving: The Riddle of the Double *Gedankenstrich*," *The Agonist*, Vol. III, Issue 1 (spring 2010). In particular, see 21–24.

seek to purge himself of terror and ruth [*Schrecken und Mitleiden*],[16] but beyond such, "*to realize in oneself* the eternal joy of becoming — that joy which also encompasses *joy in destruction*" (TI: Ancients §5). To be a tragic poet is to sanctify pain as opposed to seeking temporary comforts through evading one's suffering with linguistic ruses; it is also to recognize that not only are joy and suffering inextricably interwoven, but that joy is deeper—more profound—even than suffering.[17] This is the tragic vision *par excellence*, and it is tragic poetry that Nietzsche seeks to cultivate. As Grundlehner points out in one of the very few studies of Nietzsche's poetry, for the philosopher, "poetry was not merely occasional verse but it was defined by a critical passion for self-justification in terms of some higher meaning, some vital substance beyond the capabilities of expository or prosaic expression."[18] In opposition to the poet that is the main subject of Nietzsche's critique, it is precisely the visionary, future-minded type that I propose he writes as, or certainly strives to, and it is such a poet that enables us to bear being human as Zarathustra avows, or to be completely different kinds of human beings: to be overcoming, self-sacrificial ones who know the terrifying power of laughter.

Now, of particular concern here are the "closing melodies" or endings of *The Gay Science* and *Beyond Good and Evil* and, in addition, the integral relationship between the final aphorisms of those books and the poems that follow them, which even the two studies devoted to Nietzsche's poetry have neglected to observe.[19] If the notion of strict or pure beginnings and endings is held in question, and though Nietzsche stood in strict opposition to all systematizers, simultaneously, he was profoundly classically minded—that is, in terms of structure, in the very design and order of his books, or their architectural organization. The music of his thought. As Nietzsche himself reveals in an

---

[16] *Schrecken* and *Mitleiden* are the German terms for pity and fear, or *phobos* and *eleos*. I translate *Mitleiden* as *ruth* (as opposed to ruthless) instead of pity. Although that may not always be correct, it often is, and this suggestion may help us to hear anew—in English—what is often problematically translated as *pity* in Nietzsche's corpus. Although not commonly used nowadays, Shakespeare used the word ruth numerous times in his plays, as does Milton in his poem *Lycidas*.

[17] The extraordinary declaration by "Deep Midnight" that although the world is deep and deeper than day is aware, and its woe is deep, joy is "deeper still than misery" (Z: III.15 §3).

[18] Philip Grundlehner, *The Poetry of Friedrich Nietzsche* (Oxford: Oxford University Press, 1986), 35.

[19] Of the two major studies of Nietzsche's poetry in English, neither makes this crucial connection. See Grundlehner (*Ibid.*), and Rohit Sharma, *On the Seventh Solitude: Endless Becoming and Eternal Return in the Poetry of Friedrich Nietzsche* (London: Peter Lang, 2006).

aphorism entitled "Against the shortsighted," and this illuminating passage dramatically collapses views such as Danto's (reading Nietzsche in any indiscriminate order), Nietzsche's texts are far from a series of irregularly arranged aphorisms that can be read in any order. "Do you think this work must be a patchwork [*Stückwerk*] because I give it to you (and have to give it to you) in pieces [*Stücken*]?" (AOM §128)[20] Here, the explicit implication is that, despite the book's *Stückwerk* character, which may in part be a mask adopted out of necessity, it *is* ordered. As early as 1919 Walter Benjamin proclaimed that, "These days, the fact that an author expresses himself in aphorisms will not count for anyone as proving anything against his systematic intentions. Nietzsche, for example, wrote aphoristically, characterizing himself moreover as the enemy of system; yet he thought through his philosophy in a comprehensive and unitary manner in keeping with his guiding ideas, and in the end began to write his system."[21] And let us recall that, from the *Birth or Tragedy* to *Twilight of the Idols*, Nietzsche often praises the one and the whole over the fragment and the individual—as Zarathustra announces, emphasizing the greater significance of unity, "I compose *into one* and *bring together* what is fragment [*Bruchstücken*] and

---

[20] Translation modified — for "*Stückwerk*" Hollingdale has "fragmentary" and for "*Stücken*" he has "fragments," but this is not wholly accurate, especially since "*fragmentarisch*" is the specific German word for "fragmentary" and "*Fragmente*" (or "*Bruchstücke*") is the specific German word for "fragments." Whenever speaking of fragments, Nietzsche uses the latter two words, and his specificity here must not only be honored in translation, but in interpretation. If Hollingdale's translation isn't necessarily "wrong," but interpretive, since there is a specific word for "fragment" in German and Nietzsche does not use it in this case, the translation should be as precise as Nietzsche. Unlike *Aufgeheben*, *Stückwerk* is not rife with ambiguity or multiple meanings. There is no intractability here in terms of a corresponding word in English. Nietzsche clearly seems to deliberately differentiate his work as fragmentary *in the philosophical sense*, but that is different from stating that its structure is, in the common sense of the word, fragmentary. Here is the entire *Stück* in German: "*Meint ihr denn, es müsse Stückwerk sein, weil man es euch in Stücken giebt (und geben muss)?*" The necessity of writing in such a manner for the modern age and the modern reader, who lacks the ability for sustained concentration, may be but one reason why Nietzsche chose to give his works to us in "*Stücken*." See Jill Marsden's "Art of the Aphorism" for a slightly different view of this in *Companion to Nietzsche*, ed. Keith Ansell-Pearson (London: Wiley-Blackwell, 2006), and consider Nietzsche's own view that *Daybreak* is a book that one can "dip in and out of" — that may however be ironic.
[21] Walter Benjamin, "The Concept of Criticism in German Romanticism," *Selected Writings, Vol. I, 1913–1926* (Cambridge, MA: Belknap Press, 1996; 1999), 136.

riddle and cruel coincidence" (Z: II 20, emphasis added).[22] Only the worst readers Nietzsche notes seize bits and pieces from his texts, "dirty and confound the remainder, and revile the whole" (AOM §137).

His work's classical sense of structure is evident in numerous ways, too—most obvious, in his use of prefaces, forewords, post-scripts, and epilogues. And in the *Gay Science*, Nietzsche expresses admiration for knowing how to end things well, which he considers of particular importance: "Masters of the first rank are revealed by the fact that in great as well as small matters they know how to end perfectly, whether it is a matter of ending a melody or a thought, or the fifth act of a tragedy or of an action of state." It is only those "of the second rank" who "become restless as the end approaches and do not manage to slope into the sea in such proud and calm harmony as, for example, the mountains at Portofino—where the bay of Genoa ends its melody" (GS §281). This aphorism should attune us to the fact that the ending of the *Gay Science* is of special significance, as are the endings (and beginnings, such as for instance the generally ignored beginning of GS—the book does not begin with the first aphorism, but the prelude "Joke, Cunning, and Revenge") of all of Nietzsche's books, but let us drift slightly further afar before hearkening briefly to that closing melody.

In his detailed study of *Beyond Good and Evil*, Laurence Lampert discusses how the book's architecture is "reflected by its frame," which includes a preface and aftersong. He notes further that each of the nine chapters of the book "is composed as a coherent whole, offering an argument more latent than manifest but an argument that must be appreciated if Nietzsche's deepest aim is to be appreciated."[23] What is most conspicuously classical in the structure of the book (and this may be the case with many of his books), is how Nietzsche grounds the most fundamental thought in the exact center of each chapter. This is not to argue, as should be apparent, that Nietzsche's work is not fragmentary in the philosophical sense, or that there is closure in his thought, but that his books are very carefully constructed, that they have a larger order that is more like a constellation or magnetic field, if not a great architectural work, like the Mole Antonelliana — grand style is, as Nietzsche avows, a form of architecture,

---

[22] In BT, Nietzsche extols the community over the individual while he often praises the whole as what is highest. In GS he speaks of the one or the whole as praiseworthy, too, while in TI the whole is extolled over the individual, which N says is the "lie of the philosopher." One of the things which Nietzsche admires Goethe for is his ability to unite all into one, into an ordered whole (TI: SUM §49).

[23] Laurence Lampert, *Nietzsche's Task: An Interpretation of Beyond Good and Evil* (Connecticut: Yale University Press, 2004), 7.

which his books themselves attest to. A book is a building, thus it is to be entered through its front door, not a window on the third floor. Similarly, in his study of *Human, All Too Human*, Jonathan R. Cohen outlines how, despite its 'aphoristic' style, the book "has a unified literary structure and integrity, which are central to the communication of the book's philosophical message."[24] As Camelia Elias has observed though, the aphorism is strictly *not* a fragment, thus it isn't Nietzsche's use of aphorisms that would make the book fragmentary; in fact, as Benjamin recognized much earlier, writing aphorisms is hardly proof against systematic structures. "In terms of understanding the fragment as a performative concept, rather than as a genre," Elias explains, "the aphorism is not close to the fragment at all." Elucidating further, she states that theorists of the aphorism "make a distinction between the form and content of the aphorism at the expense of wit which figures in a subordinate relation to both the semantic and syntactic structures identified in the aphorism. […] Insofar as the aphorism thus shows a preference for form, it does not possess the same potential as the fragment to be performative."[25] This is a crucial distinction that I do not believe Nietzsche scholars such as Danto have made. When seriously considered, it will change how we read Nietzsche. Manuscript copies of Nietzsche's books also reveal that he deliberated over the order of their numbered sections, and that he arranged them with painstaking care, often changing their placement until finally settling on what he thought was the perfect arrangement, a question not only of content, but of rhythm, pace, and tempo.[26] The music of his architecture, the compositional aspect of his work, its symphonic or orchestral structure.

There is an acute subtlety here that must be tended to, for if the tempo of even a sentence is misunderstood as Nietzsche stresses, a sentence itself is misunderstood. And if even syllables are rhythmically decisive and affect a work's symmetry, as series of vowels and diphthongs color and recolor each other, how can we ignore the intricate structure of Nietzsche's works? Further,

---

[24] *Science, Culture, and Free Spirits: A Study of Nietzsche's Human, All Too Human* (Amherst: Prometheus Books, 2009).

[25] Camelia Elias, *The Fragment: Towards a History and Poetics of a Performative Genre* (Bern; Berlin: Peter Lang, 2004), 9.

[26] Aside from reading Nietzsche in his native — *Saxon* — German as Babette Babich has implored, or rather, hearing him *recited* in Saxon-inflected German, as Paolo D'Iorio has recently emphasized, what is also of utmost importance for our interpretive efforts is returning to *Nietzsche's manuscripts themselves*, for they offer illuminating insights even the published books cannot. See Paolo d'Iorio, "The Eternal Return: Genesis and Interpretation," tr. by Frank Chouraqui, *The Agonist*, Vol. III, Issue 2 (winter 2010).

if as he confessed to Rohde that his "style is a *dance*; a play of symmetries of all kinds and an overleaping and mocking of these symmetries" (writing in *Stücken* as that mockery?) which even "goes as far as the choice of vowels" (KSB July 13, 1883), ignoring the structure of his work is truly negligible. As he laments in *Beyond Good and Evil*, when "the most pronounced contrasts in style are not heard [...] the most refined artistry is *wasted*, as if on deaf people" (§246). Let us not confuse our inability to hear with the clear mastery of Nietzsche's style. Those who lack a sense for, or knowledge of, music, will then simply not hear such artistry at all. Too often, our own limitations are imposed upon thinkers whose vision is beyond our grasp, but to a composer of genius such as Mahler, that artistry was clearly evident. As Julian Johnson notes, "In a conversation with Bernard Scharlitt in 1906, Mahler is reported to have claimed about Nietzsche: 'His *Zarathustra* originated in the spirit of music; indeed it is almost symphonically conceived.' Sherzinger links this comment, a year after the completion of the *Seventh Symphony*, to a structural parallel between the Finale of the *Seventh Symphony* and a passage in Nietzsche's *Also sprach Zarathustra*. In the chapter titled 'The Seven Seals' Nietzsche evokes the idea of 'the eternal return' by reference to the form of a rondo; the rondo Finale of the *Seventh* has, interestingly, seven ritornello returns." [27] And in *Nietzsche and Music*, Liebert observes that the order which pervades Nietzsche's work is thoroughly informed by his understanding and knowledge of music: "Apparently discontinuous and even disparate, and throwing off the reader used to things laid out in chapters and paragraphs stitched together by the cadences of a linear causality, Nietzsche's work in fact obeys a principle of organization and coherence that is thematic in nature. It implies a *musical* attentiveness comparable to the one required by Wagner's works [...]." [28] We must bear this in mind when Nietzsche continually asks us if we have *heard* him correctly. In repeatedly petitioning our ears, he may be compelling us to h e a r not only the oral or synaesthetic dimension of his texts, but how they are *musically arranged*, to l i s t e n to the thematic structure of each work. [29] If the very notion of causality

---

[27] Julian Johnson, *Mahler's Voices: Expression and Irony in the Songs and Symphonies* (Oxford: Oxford University Press, 2009), 200.

[28] Georges Liebert, *Nietzsche and Music* (Chicago: University of Chicago Press, 2004), 8.

[29] There is scant to little material on the synaesthetic dimension of Nietzsche's philosophy, but it demands thorough and sustained treatments. Sarah Kofman, though not referring to it as such, briefly touches upon it (and this is the first consideration of the topic (first published in French in 1973) as far as I'm aware) in her *Nietzsche and Metaphor* (California: Stanford University Press, 1994), as does Babette Babich in her *Words in Blood, Like Flowers* (New York: SUNY Press, 2006), though her treatment is

is problematized by Nietzsche, clearly, he would not obey laws of causality in the composition of his books — his philosophical principles are embedded in the very form of how that philosophy is expressed. It is like Michelangelo's thought shaping the contour and arc of his sculptures. Babich argues that "a specifically musical temperament" is actually "required just to follow (read) Nietzsche in his textual ventures. Without a musical reading, Nietzsche offers only contradictions and logical infelicities [...]."[30] It is through tending to the musical sense of an aphorism she says that one "keeps both its subject matter and its development as parts of a whole. Thus positions, statements at variance with one another are not simply contra*dictions* but contra*puntal* [...]."[31] It is illuminating to think of larger overarching structures, too, such as the structure of a symphony, if not even of Wagner's operas, which may have been structural models for Nietzsche's works,[32] or of architectural works such as the Mole Antonelliana, when considering the design of his books, for just as his use of words and even of seemingly innocuous syntactical devices such as dashes and ellipses is geometrically precise, so too is the architectural form of his books. If Nietzsche informs us that we must be familiar with every one of his books in order to understand each individual book, and if each one of them spiders out

also brief. The only studies strictly devoted to the topic include Diana Behler, "Synaesthesia in Nietzsche's *Die Geburt der Tragödie* and Its Correlation to French and Russian Symbolism," *Carrefour de Cultures,* ed. Régis Antoine (Tübingen: Narr, 1993), 169–80, and Clive Cazeaux, "Sound and Synaesthesia in Nietzsche and Merleau-Ponty," *Proceedings of the Sound Practice Conference* (Dartington: Dartington College of Arts, 2001): 35–40. The former article only focuses on BT and suffers from a myopic understanding of the phenomenon, if not of Nietzsche; the latter, though brief and only concerned with TL, is still a rich and suggestive article even though Merleau-Ponty receives the lion's share of its focus. For the first sustained analysis of the topic, see Rainer J. Hanshe's "Nietzsche's Synaesthetic Epistemology & the Restitution of the Holistic Human," in *Nietzsche & the Becoming of Life*, eds. Vanessa Lemm & Miguel Vatter (New York: Fordham University Press, 2012).

[30] Babich, *Ibid.*, 106.

[31] And here we have perhaps yet one way of reading what have been considered contra-dictions in Nietzsche's thought. Babette Babich, "*Mousike Techne*: The Philosophical Practice of Music in Plato, Nietzsche, and Heidegger," *Between Philosophy and Poetry: Writing, Rhythm, History*, eds. Massimo Verdicchio & Robert Burch (New York; London: Continuum, 2002), 204, 178.

[32] Roger Hollinrake makes precisely this argument about Z and Wagner's operas. See his *Nietzsche, Wagner, and the Philosophy of Pessimism* (London: George Allen and Unwin, 1982; Taylor and Francis, 2009). For further explorations of this parallel, see Paul S. Loeb's *The Death of Nietzsche's Zarathustra* (Cambridge: Cambridge University Press, 2010).

of itself and into the others, stretching both backwards and forwards, anticipating, predicting, and even preceding or containing future works, each book also stands on its own as a perfected single entity and must be considered on its own terms, which is to say that each book has a structure and design that must be analyzed.[33] How is it to be entered, exited, and experienced as a wholly conceived structure? What is the experience that is being conveyed?

Now, in the "closing melodies" to the *Gay Science* and *Beyond Good and Evil*, when Nietzsche questions the value of words, of their ability to communicate thought, he seems to be thinking specifically of prose. Before his thoughts were reduced to words, he exults that they were "so colorful" and "full of thorns and secret spices," all of which caused him to sneeze and laugh. But when he mutates or *de-forms* such thoughts into prose, not only do they lose their fragrance or sensorial as well as musical dimension, they also begin to attack him: "'We can no longer stand it,' they shout at me; 'away, away with this raven-black music! Are we not surrounded by bright morning? And by soft green grass and grounds, the kingdom of the dance? Has there ever been a better hour for gaiety? Who will sing a song for us, a morning song, so sunny, so light [...]'" (GS §383). Perhaps more anxiously, he fears that, when transcribing them into prose, his thoughts are in danger of becoming truths. Immediately following these critiques, he offers us "songs," the "Songs of Prince Vogelfrei," and "From High Mountains: Aftersong."[34] There is also a similar critique of language in the finale of the third book of *Thus Spoke Zarathustra*, ending with Zarathustra's animals commanding him, "Speak no further, [...] fashion yourself a lyre, a new lyre! [...] Sing and foam over, O Zarathustra. With new songs you must heal your soul [...]" (Z: III.13 §2). After receiving this instruction, Zarathustra ceases speaking and enters into a

---

[33] As William Schaberg outlines, Nietzsche was intimately involved even in the production and design of his books and oversaw details as particular as typeface, layout, cover design, paper stock, and endpapers, as well as choosing the color of each of his books. See Schaberg, *The Nietzsche Canon: A Publication History and Bibliography* (Chicago: University of Chicago Press, 1995).

[34] Oddly, especially for a book that painstakingly analyzes structure, Lampert neglects to analyze the relationship between the final aphorism of BGE and the closing song, just as he neglects to ask *why* Nietzsche closes BGE with a poem. Kaufmann's general antipathy to Nietzsche's poetry is largely representative of the position most scholars hold. But whether one admires Nietzsche's poems, or whether they are to one's taste or not, isn't the pressing question — as emphasized throughout this essay, their very inclusion in Nietzsche's texts demands that we address them in order to analyze what precisely Nietzsche is *performing* with them and how they function within the overall architecture of his texts, etc.

conversation with his soul, which is clearly *an inaudible inner dialogue or mode of external silence*, and then *sings* his final ecstatic paeans to Life and Eternity. Thus, just as following a critique of language, *The Gay Science* and *Beyond Good and Evil* both end with songs, so too does *Zarathustra*,[35] therefore, *there is a structural parallel to the three books.— —*[36] Poems are different of course from prose, fragments, and aphorisms and are more akin to music which, unlike the former, can be given a greater multitude of interpretations — translate an aphorism and it is essentially the same from language to language, whereas Bach's *Goldberg Variations* as performed by Wanda Landowska versus Glen Gould offer exceedingly unique reconfigurations that show how transformable and free from "truth" music is. In this way then, I propose that with the songs that follow the "closing melodies" or final aphorisms of those books, the sloping into the sea in proud and calm harmony, Nietzsche attempts to surpass or overcome with them the very limits of prose, which, as he proclaims, steals the color, prickliness, and fragrance of his thoughts. Since we know that poets are "liars" for Nietzsche, that is, one specific type of poet, whatever possible truths they may produce are never in danger of becoming true, but since Nietzsche is a poet of a different order, or strives to be, that is not as much of a danger for him. Poetry for him is in part a form of power. When discussing the aftermath of the death of God, Nietzsche asks, "What festivals of atonement, what sacred games shall we have to invent? Is not the greatness of this deed too great for us? Must we ourselves not become gods simply to appear worthy of it?" (GS §125) To this last daunting question, I believe there is a clue or 'answer'—perhaps

---

[35] Taking into consideration Paul Loeb's proposal that, although, chronologically, the fourth book follows the first three, narratively, it occurs within the third. See Paul S. Loeb, "The Conclusion of Nietzsche's *Zarathustra*," *International Studies in Philosophy*, 32/3 (2000): 137–52. Even if one is not persuaded by Loeb's interpretation, the point of the structural parallel between GS, Z: III, and BGE remains, and many scholars argue that Z: III is the "real" or original finale to Z. Further, if the relationship between the three books has been recognized, since Nietzsche refers to GM as a "sonata in three movements," it is possible that it too is somehow linked, *musically*, in terms of its structure, to GS, Z, and BGE. Nietzsche was intimately involved in the design of his books and informed his publisher that he wanted BGE to look *exactly* like GM, to resemble it so precisely that "the two books must look so much alike as to be actually confused with each other." On this, see Schaberg (*ibid.*), 150.

[36] Although the parallel between two of the books has been observed, by Lampert in particular, if not others, what has been emphasized by him is that both Z and BGE end in songs. The much more specific and intriguing parallel noted above has not however to my knowledge been emphasized. Exploring this in detail is beyond the scope of this article.

response is the best word—in the aphorism on the origin of poetry in the *Gay Science*. There, Nietzsche proposes that it is specifically through rhythm that we can almost become gods, thus, poetry, or Nietzsche's very distinct type of tragic poetry, offers us a means for appearing worthy of such a sacrifice, and it perhaps enables him to say in verse what he could not say in prose, or to say it *differently*, to say it more deeply, for if joy is deeper even than woe, to end his books with songs which are in part parodic is to offer as a Provençal knight a closing melody that is more ecstatic than an aphorism, maxim, or arrow. If tragedy is born of the dithyramb as Nietzsche argues, it is perhaps out of poetry, out of a *new* dithyrambic poetry, that a tragic vision can be created or forged. And this may be precisely what Nietzsche implies with his peculiar if not perplexing claim that he is the inventor of the dithyramb— —as a poet who is a signpost to the future, he is precisely the inventor of the *new* dithyramb, the dithyramb of the future that we must create, just as we must create new myths for ourselves as did Nietzsche with *Also sprach Zarathustra*. And if, as Claudia Crawford observes, "the original function of the old dithyramb for Nietzsche was to bring real life into a sharper focus,"[37] his positive poetic type would then be the figure that stands in strict opposition to the idealistic poetic type, of which he is incisively critical. What is necessary, even in art, is bringing "real life" into as sharp a focus as possible, which is to say, shattering anthropomorphic perceptions of the world and coming as close as one can to the mode of objectivity that Nietzsche characterizes as multi-perspectival, the view of a thousand and one attentive eyes, and these it must be remembered are synesthetic eyes that hear. "Nietzsche's preferred style, once his grand *agonal* style had succeeded in propelling us into a new tragic worldview of Dionysian possibility," Crawford continues, "was to be the dithyramb, the language that Dionysian people speak when they speak to themselves" (280), or, to invoke the title of this essay, *Dionysian logos*, the logos of a poet informed by both art and science, by an optics that pierces through the fog of the human, all too human and perceives instead from cosmic perspectives, but that also includes an act of transfiguration.

[37] Claudia Crawford, "Nietzsche's Psychology and Rhetoric of World Redemption: Dionysus versus the Crucified," in *Nietzsche and Depth Psychology*, eds. Jacob Golomb, Weaver Santaniello, and Ronald Lehrer (New York: SUNY Press, 1999), 271–294. (279)

Works Cited

Ameisen, Jean-Claude. *La Sculpture du vivant. Le suicide cellulaire ou la mort créatrice* (Paris: Seuil, 2003).

Babich, Babette. "*Mousike Techne*: The Philosophical Practice of Music in Plato, Nietzsche, and Heidegger." *Between Philosophy and Poetry: Writing, Rhythm, History*. Eds. Massimo Verdicchio & Robert Burch. New York; London: Continuum, 2002.

Benjamin, Walter. "The Concept of Criticism in German Romanticism." *Selected Writings, Vol. I, 1913–1926*. Cambridge, MA: Belknap Press, 1996; 1999.

Cohen, Jonathan R. *Science, Culture, and Free Spirits: A Study of Nietzsche's Human, All Too Human*. Amherst: Prometheus Books, 2009.

Crawford, Claudia. "Nietzsche's Psychology and Rhetoric of World Redemption: Dionysus versus the Crucified." *Nietzsche and Depth Psychology*. Eds. Jacob Golomb, Weaver Santaniello, and Ronald Lehrer. New York: SUNY Press, 1999.

Elias, Camelia. *The Fragment: Towards a History and Poetics of a Performative Genre*. Bern; Berlin: Peter Lang, 2004.

Grundlehner, Philip. *The Poetry of Friedrich Nietzsche*. Oxford: Oxford University Press, 1986.

Lampert, Laurence. *Nietzsche's Task: An Interpretation of Beyond Good and Evil*. Connecticut: Yale University Press, 2004.

Liebert, Georges. *Nietzsche and Music*. Chicago: University of Chicago Press, 2004.

Löwith, Karl. *Nietzsche's Philosophy of Eternal Return*. California: University of California Press, 1997.

Nietzsche, Friedrich. *Daybreak*. Tr. by R.J. Hollingdale. Cambridge: Cambridge University Press, 1982.

---*Human, All Too Human*. Tr. by R.J. Hollingdale. Cambridge: Cambridge University Press, 1986.

---*The Gay Science*. Tr. by Walter Kaufmann. New York: Random House, 1974.

---*Thus Spoke Zarathustra*. Tr. by Graham Parkes. Oxford: Oxford University Press, 2005.

--- *Beyond Good and Evil*. New York: Random House, 1968.

--- *Twilight of the Idols*. Tr. by Duncan Large. Oxford: Oxford University Press, 1998. Tr. by R.J. Hollingdale. New York: Penguin Books, 1968.

--- *Ecce Homo*. Tr. by Duncan Large. Oxford: Oxford University Press, 2007.

--- *Briefwechsel Kritische Gesamtausgabe*. Eds. Giorgio Colli, Mazzino Montinari. Berlin: Walter de Gruyter, 1977.

http://nietzschesource.org

Paz, Octavio. *The Bow and the Lyre*. New York: McGraw Hill, 1973.

Pothen, Philip. *Nietzsche and the Fate of Art*. London: Ashgate, 2002.

Schaberg, William. *The Nietzsche Canon: A Publication History and Bibliography*. Chicago: University of Chicago Press, 1995.

Schlegel, Friedrich. *On the Study of Greek Poetry*. New York: SUNY Press, 2001.

How to Sing the Practical Sound of the Enigma
Nietzsche's Zarathustra for Everyday Life

Alessio Tommasoli

Most of Nietzsche's philosophy is expressed through a particular style of writing made of cryptic lyricism and symbolic images. Such a unique philosophical expression makes Nietzsche's thought a "tool" that requires the mental elaboration of the reader, so to engage him in a hermeneutic interpretation that starts from everyday life.

Therefore Nietzsche's reader seems to be more than a listener that just hears some words reading a book; he is a listener that feels the need to sing the words he reads. That is because he guesses that the sense of these words is not in their possible meanings, but in the sensations that they give him.

Anyway it does not mean that Nietzsche's philosophy is open to all sorts of interpretations. That is because it is rooted in a specific matter that is the concept. The time-space dimension of human "*hic et nunc*" indeed always refers to a theory and vice versa, so that philosophy is an existential practice and the existential condition is a philosophy.

In Nietzsche's production the concept has a double role of importance: on the one hand, it pulls together the fragments of his cryptic expression (such as the aphorisms), and, on the other one, it is fragmented itself, to show all its possible perspectives. If the first one is a theoretical approach, the latter is practical, because in this way the concept allows the reader to find in itself all the existential possibilities.

As Gilles Deleuze wrote, [1] every concept has always a "conceptual character", that is a figure able to embody and perform it through his actions and his life. It is exactly the way through which philosophy, according to Deleuze, is rooted in an immanent dimension, translating its theory in the practice of life.

---

[1] Deleuze, G., Guattari, F., *What is Philosophy?*, translated by Tomlinson H, Burchill G, London; New York : Verso, 1994.

Nevertheless, on the opposite point of view, the character is the medium between every narrative work of art and the audience (or the reader). It allows this latter to enter into the work and live it in first person.

Thus Zarathustra is Nietzsche's conceptual character of a specific idea, the "will to power". Through Zarathustra indeed the reader lives the existential need that only this concept can help to solve, with no meaningful words to listen, but with a will to sing the sound of its enigma as if it was an Opera.

Act One:

1. Ouverture

Zarathustra is not just the conceptual character of *Thus Spoke Zarathustra*, but of Nietzsche's entire philosophy. That is because some key issues of the "will to power" concept seem to appear already in his essay *The Birth of Tragedy* (1872). Here the reader can find an opening symphony that introduces him to the atmosphere in which action will happen through the main themes: it is the first part of the opera that is called the "Ouverture".

It is an essential part, therefore it is impossible for the reader to sing Zarathustra's sound if he does not set an original existential matter: "How can we stand the truth without denying life?" The answer to this question passes through two other conceptual characters that could be somehow the forefathers of Zarathustra, Dionysus and Apollo. The dialogue between these two characters indeed allows a reply to the "Silenic truth" according to which the best thing for the human is utterly beyond its reach: not to have been born, not to *be*, to be been born *AS nothing*, not *being*, being *nothing*. However the second best thing for you is: "to die soon".[2]

In this way, the reader can feel the deepest existential trouble, the one that belongs to the human nature, and find at the same time an answer: the Attic tragedy, that gives an ethical content to the aesthetic form. As Nietzsche writes indeed, the solution is already a "will" that desires the human condition, that is to say a behaviour that accepts the plural, dynamic, chaotic and contradictory whole of existence: "So stormily does the 'Will', on the level of the Apolline, demand this existence, so utterly at one with it does Homeric man feel himself to be, that even his lament turns into a song in praise of being."[3]

---

[2] It is a translation from Eudemos, a dialogue of Aristotle of which only fragments survive. Nietzsche F., *The Birth of Tragedy*, edited by Geuss, R., Speirs, R., Cambridge University Press, 1999, p. 23.

[3] Ibid, p. 24.

When Nietzsche's study of the Greeks addresses the matter of truth, ethical content and aesthetic form (such as Apollonian and Dionysian) mean to be the dualism of knowledge. In this way the question changes in: "What is the truth?". Is it the metaphysical truth, as *adaequatio rei et intellectus*? Or instead is the truth as "disclosure" of the one reality hidden under the multiplicity of perception?

In front of such a question, the correspondence between the art dualism and the knowledge dualism allows the reader to feel his own dualism based on the antagonism of the Dionysian instinct with the Apollonian one. That is to say that the reader, by virtue of his natural human dualism, feels to embody with one of these two different conceptual characters, exactly Dionysus or Apollo, so that he is exposed to the dangerous unbalance of his own instincts.

On the one hand, indeed, the Dionysian instinct is an unbalance in which the human being is the witness of a brutal and fleeting disclosure of truth. Therefore he lives the truth for a very short time through a debauched moment of inebriation in which he reconciles with Nature and with the god, but he loses himself. Human being is overwhelmed by the violent whole of truth.[4]

On the other hand, the apollonian instinct is an unbalance in which human being lives the disclosure of truth through the artistic dream or the theoretical rationality. Therefore he lives the truth as a static and closed individualization that is, according to Nietzsche, the degeneration of the Attic tragedy whose representatives are Socrates and Euripides. The human being watches a single portion of truth from the safe distance of the symbol.[5]

Thus the answer that the Greeks give to the Silenic truth is not the rational rigidity of apollonian condition, nor the unbridled dissolution of the Dionysian condition. It is indeed their balance which makes the dialogue they have in the drama of the Attic tragedy: "Thus drama is the Apollonian embodiment of Dionysiac insights and effects."[6]

The Dionysian inebriation and the Apollonian form represent at the same time two opposite aesthetic expressions and two opposite forms of knowledge of truth. Thus it is just the dialogue between these opposite ones that makes the best truth's knowledge. It is quite a negative dialectics: the human being is dragged into the whole unbearable truth that overwhelms him; but he can set himself in the right distance to watch it from the outside. In this way human

---

[4] Ibid, p. 29.
[5] Ibid, p. 92.
[6] Ibid, p. 44.

being can have a critical consciousness that allows him to make a clear analysis of truth.[7]

In conclusion, Dionysus and Apollo are the first conceptual characters of the "will to power" concept, because they embody the two different worldview's (*Weltanschauung*) perspectives that Zarathustra goes beyond. Therefore the reader can identify with an existential condition in which he feels lost in his life, so much overwhelmed from what he lives that he cannot understand it ("lived" by his own existential condition); but he can identify too with another existential condition in which he feels lost in himself, so far from what he lives that he cannot relate to them ("detached" from his own existential condition).

In this way the reader can listen to the first note of the opening symphony of the Zarathustra's sound, because this latter is the conceptual character of the "will to power" concept whose basis is the balance between Dionysus and Apollo. Therefore they are two "spirits", as Nietzsche writes, two extreme parts of the same subject, the human being, and Zarathustra represents the human being who goes beyond his own dualism, who controls and uses their opposition as a tool to find an answer to the Silenic truth. For this reason Zarathustra is the *Übermensch*.

Even if the reader can now listen to the first note of the *Ouverture* of the Zarathustra's opera through *The Birth of Tragedy*, he cannot listen to the whole sound of *Thus Spoke Zaratustra*'s enigma without another key note: the "gay science" concept. In Nietzsche's philosophy, indeed, the conceptual character transition from Dionysus (and Apollo) to Zarathustra cannot become true without the conceptual character of the Greek man that embodies the "gay science" concept. Therefore such a character has an originary self-consciousness in which he understands to be an individual and detached part of a Whole, so to get a feeling of insignificance and, at the same time, a liberating joy.

In this way the reader can re-emerge from the existential condition that overwhelms him, or he can re-conquer it if he feels completely detached, because the Greek man consciously accepts the human condition, so to be happy through it—and not in spite of it.[8] It is what Nietzsche calls the "gay science": a way through which man can handle the truth, living in a vital and positive pessimism that is the awareness of his human limit.

---

[7] In this way, it seems possible to change the word 'beauty' with the word 'truth' in some passages of *Human, All Too Human*, for example in "The slow arrow of beauty", Nietzsche F, *Human, All Too Human*, Translated by Hollingdale, R.J., Cambridge University Press, 1996, p. 81.

[8] Ibid, pp. 100–106.

Therefore the conceptual character of the Greek man is the complete transition from the Dionysus/Apollo aesthetics to the ethics, because such a conscience is the weight and the privilege of the human being's responsibility of his own strength and action. Nevertheless it is a responsibility resulted from what distinguishes the man from the animals, that is the weight and the privilege of memory and the consequent ability to dominate time.

A man who does not get such a conscience is dominated by the events that happen to him, because he does not live in a specific dimension of space and time. Anyway Nietzsche writes that the memory cannot exist without the oblivion, as the responsibility cannot exist without choice: man looks at the oblivious animals and understands that he could live like them, if only he would choose it. [9]

Thus the reader of *The Gay Science* can understand that he has the key choice of memory's responsibility and freedom, giving up the passivity of the oblivion. He can find indeed a self-consciousness that is exactly the awareness of his temporal essence. He can understand that he is living in a history made of a specific space and time (*hic et nunc*) and that he can dominate it through the memory. That is the reason why such a conscience gives to the man the enthusiasm for his ability to act that Nietzsche calls "gay science". [10]

The transition from the conceptual characters of Dionysus and Apollo to the Greek man offers a deeper answer to the Silenic truth and extends the reader's perspective on the human condition's trouble. Hence when the reader of *The Gay Science* is identified with the Greek man, he can listen to a second crucial note that will lead him towards the whole sound of Zarathustra's enigma, the ethical note.

Nevertheless the reader has to listen to a third note before he gets the full opening symphony of the opera. Indeed he has to pass through another matter that born once he got the conscience of time and it is the question: what is time for me?

It is a question that arises from the same *The Gay Science*, a sort of open conclusion of this book that ends where something else has to start. The answer is relevant, because it can make the conscience of time as the most precious gift or the cruellest sentence: as in the fragment named "The Heaviest Weight". [11]

---

[9] Nietzsche, Friedrich. *On the Advantage and Disadvantage of History for Life*. Indianapolis: Hackett Pub. Co, 1980.

[10] Nietzsche F, *The Gay Science*, edited by Williams B, Cambridge University Press, 2001.

[11] Ibid, p. 191.

In front of such a dreadful image, the Greek man turns slowly into the new conceptual character, Zarathustra. The transition happens when an idea of time as "eternal recurrence" of the same takes place that makes the "gay science" concept no longer useful. The Zarathustra figure indeed arises together with the need of a new concept, the "will to power", that can answer a new existential question about time: how can I dominate time, if it dominates me and swallows my existence through its continuous repetition of instants that are equal to themselves?

It is the last note of the opening symphony of the Zarathustra's opera. The *Overture* is accomplished because the reader is inside the atmosphere of the opera through his ability to listen.

2. Aria

Nietzsche's answer to the new existential question about time lies inside of *Thus Spoke Zarathustra*. And naturally it is expressed by the conceptual character of Zarathustra who shares his vision with some sailors, as they are the worshippers of the enigmas. It is exactly the chapter titled "The Vision and the Enigma".[12]

Here the reader finds the real sound of the opera, the "Aria": it is the lyric melody sung by the lead voice of the main character, Zarathustra, and it allows the reader to listen to the key theme of the enigma. Zarathustra's monologue indeed offers to the reader a concrete image of the latter and of the idea of eternal recurrence of the same: the dwarf. Nevertheless the dwarf is not just an image, but is a conceptual character as well as Zarathustra. It is exactly the opponent of Zarathustra, as well as the eternal recurrence concept that it embodies is the antagonist of the will to power concept embodied by Zarathustra.

Therefore the dwarf is the same demon of *The Gay Science* that here places the burden on Zarathustra's impetus towards his self-determination. Anyway here the demon does not burden anymore on a simple man (the ancient Greek man), but on an *Übermensch* who is not scared of it and who despises it indeed. In this way the eternal recurrence is no longer the "heaviest weight", but a wrong perspective towards which the shepherd's face is transfigured by a smile.

---

[12] Nietzsche, F., *Thus Spoke Zarathustra*, editor Del Caro, A, Pippin, R.B., Cambridge University Press, 2006, pp. 124-127.

3. Duetto

The reader is naturally dazed and confused by Zarathustra's words, because he listened to a pure enigma. But he listens to a sound so harmonious that he can sense something deep, such an intuition of a concept that he cannot completely rationally get. It is a sort of aesthetic comprehension of a special perspective about the time that dominates him: do not escape time to refuse it and do not think to change its nature, but do accept it and do want it, so to convert the trouble for the condemnation into a pleasure.

In this way the reader can sense the dramatic vision of the shepherd's bite to the snake as a specific behaviour: a way to rule the eternal recurrence governing himself inside the existential condition of the eternal recurrence. Thus the reader can feel the need of an ethical decision in which the action is full of responsibility and freedom.

It is now the time for the "Duetto" of the opera, where Zarathustra expands his voice to alternate it, to intertwine it and to connect it with the reader's voice that is now instinctively trying to sing the sound of the enigma: it is in the chapter named "On Self-Overcoming".[13]

Hence the will to power is such a movement of creation that the reader shall act inside the temporal condition of the eternal recurrence of the same: he shall seize the Instant and he shall want it, and he shall destroy the Instant to go beyond it, and then he shall want the Instant back, in a personal brand new perspective.

4. Arioso

In this way the reader finds the rhythm of the Zarathustra's sound, the rhythm of time that keeps coming back, again and again, but under his control, by his will and his decision. It is a sound whose artistic form expresses the dynamism of the same human existence and drives it to its limit: to want the pain in order to turn it into a pleasure. Here is the "Arioso" of the opera, a moment in which the form of the sound is recited in a way that highlights the passionate movement of the words: it is the Thus Spoke Zarathustra's chapter titled "The Sleepwalker Song".[14]

Nevertheless, in the latter words mentioned, Zarathustra is speaking to some "higher men", that is to say some person who has gone beyond "the small virtues, the small sagacities, the infinite sense of respect, the rolling swarm of ant's small business, the miserable pleasure, the happiness of the majority".

---

[13] Ibid, pp. 88-90.
[14] Ibid, §10 and §11, pp. 261-263.

Consequently Zarathustra is speaking to the ears of a specific reader, the one who tried to sing his sound. Even if he did not do so well, he is now an active reader who overcame his listener passive condition. He is a reader who made a distinction between his existential condition and himself, who can watch critically what happens from the right distance, who arose from the engulfment of what occurred or who reconciled his own detachment.

5. *Concertato*

Hence Zarathustra can now sing together with such a reader, because this latter is now the ethical man who is "free from" and to whom he can teach how to be "free to" – do, act, make, create. Therefore Zarathustra can now leads the singing of the will to power together with some "higher men" to whom he shows the route towards the *Übermensch*. It is such a fairy-tale taught by a father to his child, through which he explains to him that he has to grow up and pass through the "The Three Metamorphoses".[15] Here is the "Concertato" of the opera, the moment in which some lead vocals sing together in a difficult game, so to express the dramatic and psychological relevance of the action.

The difficult game that the lead vocals are playing here expresses concretely the hard route towards the "will to power" concept and shows the chorus of the whole opera, as a refrain that was born in *The Gay Science* and repeats stronger in *Thus Spoke Zarathustra*: "You shall become what you are".[16]

Such an imperative is a real, practical commendation that supports the whole opera, as a chorus does. The reader can now sing the sound of the enigma as a single part of this chorus, not just thoughtlessly following its rhythm, but acting the words that it sings. Thus, singing this sound for the reader means to accept his own changing identity (self-consciousness) and to want it; it means to produce something from the indeterminateness through the creativity of his own act; it means to get an answer to the ancestral matter ("How can we stand the truth without denying the life?") and to all its possible variations.

Above all, singing the sound of Zarathustra's enigma means to get the opportunity to dominate time and to want everything, the future, the present and the past time too: "You must want what you have been and what you are in order to be what you want".

---

[15] Ibid, pp. 16-17.
[16] Nietzsche, F., *The Gay Science*, cited, p. 152.

6. Finale

However, even if he sang the whole sound, the reader cannot be considered as an *Übermensch*. He is a "higher man", it is sure, he is close to be "the son" of Zarathustra, but he is still restrained inside his human condition. That is because, even if he reached the balance for a while, he is still vulnerable to the imbalance and to some moralistic ideas, like Pity and Compassion. It is what happens in the final chapter of *Thus Spoke Zarathustra*, "The Sign": the higher men are still sleeping and dreaming the sound of Zarathustra as some drunken songs and they do not like the entire and complex opera.[17]

It seems to be the "Finale" of the opera, the closing moment in which several voices can meld together like goes here, where Zarathustra's voice melds with the narrator's voice, so to give an impressive conclusion that makes the reader once more dazed and confused.

7. Intermezzo

But while the theater's curtain falls, it starts to play a musical interlude that let the reader understand that the sound of the enigma continues and the opera is about to go on. Thus it was just the final moment of the first act that is connected to the second act through an intermission, as a prelude that is the "Intermezzo" of the opera: "Thinking, feeling, willing in all living beings. What is a pleasure but; an excitation of the feeling of power by an obstacle (even more strongly by rhythmic obstacles and resistances) – so it swells up. Thus all pleasure includes pain—if the pleasure is to be very great, the pains must be very protracted and the tension of the bow tremendous".[18]

The reader is surprised because these are not the words of Zarathustra, even if it is still the sound of the enigma. In such a symphonic interlude, Nietzsche is the narrator himself, so that he does not need any conceptual character and says his words directly to the reader, as if he looks at this latter figure as a higher man quite ready to overcome his nature.

Hence it should not astonish the reader that the book from which this sound comes is exactly named "The Will to Power", the concept that now he should represent as the new conceptual character. However "The Will to Power" is just the name of a controversial collection of some of Nietzsche's

---

[17] Nietzsche, F., *Thus Spoke Zarathustra*, cited, p. 264–266.
[18] Nietzsche, F., *The Will to Power*, translated by Kaufmann W, Hollingdale, R.J., Vintage Books, 1968, p. 347.

notes and aphorisms written during the psychotic breakdown of his last years, therefore it has a fragmented and confused form.

However the surprising discovery of a second act of the Nietzsche's philosophy opera, places the reader on the right route towards the *Übermensch*, so that he cannot refuse it and he needs help to fix the broken sound of the enigma in order to set up its pieces and finally sing a complete sound.

Act Two:

8. Ouverture

Such help is offered by Martin Heidegger's essay "Nietzsche".[19] Indeed it explains the "will to power" concept in an ethical way as the connection between freedom and necessity. Therefore the deep and complex sound of Nietzsche's opera seems to be closer to the reader and his life since the "Overture" of the second act, where the atmosphere of the action hosts him in so direct a way that he can feel attacked. Heidegger indeed talks about a courage that fights cowardliness and ignorance, and that makes eternity a human choice through the will to want every instant on which it is built. [19]

Where the reader feels choked by an inevitable duty or by a need to which he does not belong, he understands that he can change perspective when he wants what it is, so to become the ruler of what it is. The need to accept the temporal dimension of the eternal recurrence makes freedom. And it is not just the idea according to which every choice that has been made (or not made) has some consequences. Such a freedom indeed is the idea that every choice concerns itself to a present time, to an instant that the higher man must actively want it and actively create it, as if it would repeat forever.

9. Aria.

Hence it is an ethical freedom because it concerns a particular question: "is this choice for yesterday, for today, for tomorrow, in the eternity?". It is the "Aria" of the second act, as the melody sung by the lead voice of the actual conceptual character: the reader.

This latter sings it because he wants to live the accident that he is living, both positive and negative, 'beyond Good and Evil', in order to become conscious of himself, to be responsible and to be free to act over this accident.

---

[19] Heidegger, M, *Nietzsche, Vol. 1: The Will to Power as Art, Vol. 2: The Eternal Recurrance of the Same*, translated by Farrell Krell, D., Harperone, San Francisco, 1991, p. 393.

For example, the reader could live the existential condition of a judgment call and he could be afraid of the negative consequences of such a call. The melody he is singing here is the will to power's melody and it does not prevent one to be afraid, nor to be brave. Indeed it allows one to accept the fear as something indivisible from bravery, because both are basic parts of the choice.

Thus the reader can finally understand what he is singing, as if he came out of the cave and sang a single meaningful song, no more asleep and no more drunk.

10. Duetto

According to Nietzsche, the Will is based on the dualism between two feelings, "rage" and "hate". As Heidegger explains, they are not similar and they are contradictory singular parts of one negative dialectical process whose general elements are "appetite" and "passion".

Appetite is the reader's continuous dynamism, that is, the constant movement of dissipation: it is a relentless overcoming of himself and of his experience, like a 'going beyond himself'. As an appetite, rage attacks and excites us so hard to push us out of ourselves, so then we are not masters of ourselves anymore. Hence in such a being out of ourselves we miss something and it is an unpleasant (*ungut*) sensation. Therefore Heidegger calls rage *Un-wille*, not-will, that is an indignation in which we totally lose ourselves.[20]

On the opposite, passion is the reader's conservation of himself, the preservation of his own full complexity as a communion of his past experiences in a unity. Passion is the gathering of these latter in the determination of an individuality. As a passion, hate attacks us like rage does, but in a different way, because it is something alive that we have already inside us. Exactly like love, hate fills and unifies our whole being in a lasting condition. That is why hate can grow up and can erode our being. Hate and love are not blind, fleeting and fragile as rage and falling in love, but they are lucid, stable and strong. That is because they are passions through which we take hold in ourselves and we get control of the entity around us and inside us.[21]

Here is the "Duetto" of the second act of the opera, a moment in which the reader, as the conceptual character, has a melodic dialogue. Anyway, differently from the first act, such a dialogue does not take place between two characters, but it goes on as an intimate dialogue of the reader with himself. That is because

---

[20] Ibid, p. 55-58.
[21] Ibid, p. 59-61

he is dual and his nature is the changing result of a negative dialectical process between Appetite and Passion.

Therefore the reader makes an incredible sound here in which he deeply alternates, intertwines and connects two different voices of his own. In this moment of the opera the lead voice of the character indeed splits and becomes two voices, but just to turn again into one, harmonious, aware and stronger than before.

11. *Recitativo and Arioso*

Hence in the current moment of the opera the lead voice of the character fills up the whole atmosphere, because the reader embodies the will to power through his own existential experience, as one of the deepest 'accidents' that he can live in his life, that is, love.

It is a very particular moment of the opera in which "Recitativo" and "Arioso" join together in order to involve the sound of the opera in a speech that enhances the passionate nature of the will to power. Here the reader understands through his own flesh how concrete such a philosophical concept can be and how deeply it lies in his own, so much that he does not express it through some words.

It is a thought indeed that he whispers silently to his own: Love is not the need of another person, nor the satisfaction of another person's need; but, yes, Love is offering him an 'extra' of yourself, it is giving him the existential fullness of yourself that does not requires any biological necessity.

In such a thought Appetite and Passion join together and make the feeling of Love an existential equivalent of the will to power concept, because the Appetite's 'joy' and 'falling in love' take their right place as parts of the whole that is the more complex determination of Passion's 'Love'. In this way the reader gets the will to power as something completely different from the 'necessity' and he gets it indeed as a free 'gift',[22] a squander.

12. *Concertato*

Hence the will to power lies on the balance between Appetite and Passion. However they are something more than just two feelings: and the reader understands their nature only since he gets their dialectical relation: this latter

---

[22] In this sense, Georges Bataille's concept of 'dépense' can offer a good clarification, because its example is the particular articulation of the 'gift' as the 'potlach'. Bataille, G., *La Notion de Dépense*, Nouvelles Editions Lignes, 2011.

does not produce any synthesis that would impoverish the thesis and the antithesis, but indeed it enhances both. Their dialectical movement makes a human being able to continuous fling beyond himself through the continuous mastery of himself, such an incessant overstepping of becoming and a resolute conservation of being.

Here is the "Concertato" of the second act in which the reader is a higher man that sings through a complex game of voices which lie in his mind as thoughts or go out in words, voices that remain silent psychological poses or become actions. His voice comes and goes, moves and remains still in a dialectical sound where any motion does not exist without a stillness that includes it.

Thus the reader sing a sound that continually points him towards brand new experiences keeping constantly the awareness of all his past experiences. The main theme is the same of the first act's final moment, a future built on the present instant that includes the whole past whose melody plays: "You must want what you have been in order to be what you want". But the character has definitely changed in this second act, so that the melody he sings seems to draw an image of the will to power concept clearer than before, because now it passes through the best human expression, the feeling, and become 'Big Passion' that is the Nietzsche's Will to Power. It is a quiet movement—not for insecurity or slowness—for the self-confidence of controlling yourself that leaps you towards other things and keeps them under the control of your actions.[23]

13. Finale

In this way, the conceptual character of the reader fulfils the whole opera through his own singing, as well as the human being fulfils the will to power concept through his action. Hence it is the realization of Nietzsche's philosophy in the agreement of the tension between Aesthetics and Ethic.

Therefore the will to power manifests itself in Nietzsche's opera as the internalisation and the expression of the reader, that makes the concept a feeling, as the 'Big Passion', and an artwork, as the 'Big Style'. The Attic Tragedy of the first act indeed becomes an actual moment of the second act, exactly the "Finale". That is because the Attic Tragedy here is fulfilled by the reader's singing. Through this singing he plays the contradiction between the Dionysian and the Apollonian spirits: the reader goes beyond himself maintaining himself in a quiet control of the incessant dynamism of life, as well as the Dionysian's creative inebriation takes a form from the Apollonian's tangible beauty.

---

[23] Ibid, p. 59-65.

54

Here is the majestic moment of the opera in which all its conceptual characters sing together the whole sound of the enigma, as if it were the existence itself. So that the different voices of Dionysus, of Apollo, of the Greek man, of Zarathustra and of the reader too, become just one impressive lead voice or a chorus that joins the imposing playing of a symphonic orchestra. Such a majestic chorus enhances the opera as the most clear form of the human state through which a human being can watch around him and become self-conscious. Their singing is the glorification of the opera itself, because it is art and art is the most transparent form of the will to power.[24]

Hence the reader is an essential part of an art composition that, through its aesthetic quality, goes beyond itself and reaches an ethical quality based on the will to overstep and preserve at the same time the 'becoming' through the 'being'.

14. Intermezzo

The theater's curtains fall slowly on the last note of the collective symphony that prolongs itself until the curtains completely darken the stage. All the characters leave the proscenium, the orchestra ceases and the sound of the enigma seems to be over. The reader, like a theatre's spectator, stands up to reach the exit and comes back to his everyday life.

Nevertheless, when he is out, under the sun's rays of his history and the clouds of his country, in front of the wind of time and space he lives, he can still listen to that sound. As if the melody he sang was an unbreakable refrain full of sense that accompanies every act he makes. As if the will to power were a benign virus that infects all his actions. As if he were no longer reader, no longer spectator and no longer man; but a creator, an artist indeed, a higher man, for sure. As if the opera were not over at all and if it went on in a third act on the stage of his life, in which he could maybe become, finally, an *Übermensch*.

Works Cited

Deleuze, G., Guattari F, *What is Philosophy?*, translated by Tomlinson, H., Burchill, G., London; New York : Verso, 1994.

Heidegger, M., *Nietzsche, Vol. 1: The Will to Power as Art, Vol. 2: The Eternal Recurrence of the Same*, translated by Farrell Krell D, Harperone, San Francisco, 1991.

Nietzsche F., *The Birth of Tragedy*, edited by Geuss, R., Speirs, R., Cambridge University Press, 1999.

---

[24] Ibid, p. 130-150.

Nietzsche, F., *Human, All Too Human*, Trans. by Hollingdale R J, Cambridge University Press, 1996.

Nietzsche, F., *The Gay Science*, edited by Williams B, Cambridge University Press, 2001.

Nietzsche, F., *On the Advantage and Disadvantage of History for Life*, Hackett Publishing, Indianapolis; Cambridge, 1980.

Nietzsche. F., *Thus Spoke Zarathustra*, editor Del Caro A, Pippin R B, Cambridge University Press, 2006.

Nietzsche, F., *The Will to Power*, translated by Kaufmann, W., Hollingdale, R.J., Vintage Books, 1968.

Zarathustra's Overman, or the Suggestive Power of Metaphor

Dirk R. Johnson

Zarathustra is both Nietzsche's most famous and most allusive text. It appears almost without precedent in the philosopher's corpus, and it has led to an interesting breakdown in his readership. Some scholars are drawn to it and attempt to unlock its riddles or propose sweeping interpretations of its hidden messages. Others are unsure of what do with it. These readers gravitate either toward the more systematically argued early works or to the later, post-*Zarathustra* writings.

No matter what one makes of *Zarathustra*, it is undeniable that its three central metaphors—the overman, the eternal return, the will to power—have exerted an inordinate influence on Nietzsche reception. In many ways, those metaphors shape the perception of Nietzsche in the popular imagination, and they cling to his philosophy, despite the fact that two of them, the overman and the eternal return, occur almost exclusively within this one text alone.[1]

In the reception of this work, readers have been taken in by the suggestive power of the metaphors, and they see *Zarathustra* as the platform from which Nietzsche first presents a visionary future for humanity. This view is misguided and deserves to be challenged.

I will argue this from three different perspectives. First, I will examine the narrative strategies of the text. The latter often get neglected for a style of interpretation that accepts the prophetic tenor of the work. Second, I will look at Nietzsche's increasingly critical understanding of "man" prior to this text, and in those that follow, to show that a higher humanity—that what the overman is meant to embody—is an awareness that Nietzsche rejects. Finally, I will disentangle the notion of the eternal return from the overman to show that

---

[1] The bulk of "overman" references appears in *Zarathustra* and in the fragments written during its composition, from Summer 1882 to Fall 1883 (Marie-Luise Haase, "Der Übermensch in *Also Sprach Zarathustra* und im Zarathustra Nachlass 1882-1885." *Nietzsche Studien* 13 (1984), 229). Only isolated references to it occur in later published works or fragments, and some of the most prominent appear in connection with *Zarathustra*, in *Ecce Homo*. This underscores how intimately this particular metaphor is linked to the text and its narrative strategies.

instead of belonging together, as many scholars assume, the thought of the eternal return renders the overman superfluous.

The Suggestive Power of Metaphor

German soldiers in World War I, it is said, rushed into the trenches with copies of *Zarathustra* in their breast pockets. For a society disenchanted with traditional Christianity, *Zarathustra* became an ersatz Bible that filled the void left by the "death of God." The ideas presented in Nietzsche's other texts were meant to force a reckoning with the nihilism of the modern age, and many early readers believed that *Zarathustra* envisioned a future human type, or overman, who would redeem mankind from nihilism. For this wartime cohort, Nietzsche's *Zarathustra* became synonymous with Nietzsche himself.

In the modern era, Heidegger's ambitious and influential reading of *Zarathustra* artfully subsumed Nietzsche's other works under his interpretation of *Zarathustra*, thereby privileging this particular text. Heidegger apotheosized its central metaphors and constructed a philosophy congenial to his project of subverting Western metaphysics. Heidegger's "Nietzsche" came to be identified with the grand doctrines of the overman, the eternal return, and the will to power. Thus, Nietzsche continued to be seen in the suggestive light of metaphors that appeared almost exclusively in this one text.

Today, the text divides scholarship into two camps—those who are drawn to its allusiveness and those others who are uncomfortable with its singular style, content, and mode of presentation. In part, this divide is due to the wholly uncritical enthusiasm with which the first generation of readers had greeted *Zarathustra*, a response now regarded with skepticism.

But it also due to the sustained power of its central metaphors, which can overpower, unsettle or frighten with their limitless suggestiveness. Readers, who can align the *Genealogy of Morals*, for example, with their contemporary interest in moral psychology, biology, or epistemology, retreat in embarrassment from the "visionary" *Zarathustra*. And yet, undeniably, the same critical intelligence that composed the *Gay Science* or *Beyond Good and Evil* also produced *Zarathustra*. Indeed, the Nietzsche of *Zarathustra* is not a new or a different Nietzsche, but one who subtly and consciously played with his audience's cultural expectations by both engaging and undermining them at the same time.

Zarathustra's Narrative Strategies

In recent years, scholars have increasingly analyzed the middle-period and post-*Zarathustra* texts from the point of view of style and language. This mode of reading is a welcome departure, for it moves us away from seeing

Nietzsche's writings as mere carriers for specific ideas and principles, such as perspectivism or the question of value, which can be neatly parsed. Instead, readers have begun to appreciate that Nietzsche was a master stylist, who conveyed his meanings *in strong part* through language and style. This perspective challenges many of our pre-conceived notions of "philosophy."[2] In the Anglo-Saxon community, the analytic approach in the academy has shaped this perception, and it comes as no surprise, then, that interpreters sympathetic to the analytical tradition have most resisted *Zarathustra*.[3]

A corrective to the latter development has come primarily from the German-speaking world. Here the texts are read in the original language, where one can more fully appreciate questions of style and linguistic nuance. To name one example, Werner Stegmaier's *Nietzsches Befreiung der Philosophie* (De Gruyter 2012)[4] analyzes the Fifth Book of *Gay Science* on the basis of its stylistic composition. Stegmaier reveals to what extent Nietzsche in this work conveys his "philosophy" through language, rhetorical devices such as ellipses, and even through his use of punctuation. He also shows how carefully Nietzsche crafts each passage and strategically places it within the text as a whole.

At this point, many scholars can agree that Nietzsche was a skilled literary craftsman, who was not only versed in the arsenal of ancient rhetoric—he was a highly learned and respected classicist, after all—but who meticulously composed his texts to achieve maximum effect—both in terms of personal experience and level of awareness. This holds true for both the pithy epigrams

---

[2] One of the major postwar English-language studies of Nietzsche after Walter Kaufmann was Arthur Danto's 1965 monograph with the telling title, *Nietzsche as Philosopher* (New York: Columbia University Press). Danto felt the need to burnish Nietzsche's credibility as a philosopher by showing how many of his concerns anticipated analytic positions. He even suggested that Nietzsche would have spoken (written) more clearly if only he had understood some of the things we now know today: "because we know a good deal more philosophy today, I believe it is exceedingly useful to see his analyses in terms of logical features which he was unable to make explicit, but toward which he was unmistakably groping" (Danto, 13)! Nothing better encapsulates the inherent skepticism and unease (disdain?) with which analytic philosophers approach Nietzsche's language.

[3] A notable exception is Paul Loeb's *The Death of Nietzsche's Zarathustra* (Cambridge: Cambridge University Press, 2010). Loeb combines an analytic approach with a sensitivity toward the literary features of *Zarathustra*.

[4] For my recent review of Stegmaier's monograph, see *The Agonist* 11:1, 31-34 (Fall 2017).

and for lengthier sustained passages. He conveys his meanings only *in part* through direct communication of a specific point; another major part is transmitted through subtle contrast, artful juxtaposition, rhythm and tempo and—perhaps more than anything else—through a sophisticated use of irony, which should prevent us from taking any discrete piece of text at face value.

Scholars are beginning to recognize these strategies in Nietzsche's more systematically argued texts, i.e., those pre- and post-*Zarathustra*. But surprisingly, in the case of *Zarathustra*, the same level of literary discernment and critical awareness of textual strategies recedes in favor of an analysis of the metaphors, and the suggestive power of its central images seem to overwhelm many interpreters. In addition, the oracular tone of the text, combined with Nietzsche's choice of an ancient prophet to be his central character, prejudges many readers.[5]

Even if there is a growing consensus that one should interpret *Zarathustra* with greater critical discernment—e.g., that one should read Nietzsche's prophet against the grain and not merely as a naïve mouthpiece of its author—that awareness does not extend to its alleged "teachings." Namely, scholars may now recognize that inherent to *Zarathustra* is his failure to disseminate his message, and this failure is built into the narrative structure. But this same critical awareness does not extend to the metaphors. The latter continue to be extracted from *Zarathustra* and used as a lens through which to view his other works. These metaphors, like giant balloons, have become unmoored from this one text, have taken on a life of their own, and inform interpretations of Nietzsche's work as a whole.

---

[5] Nietzsche portrays the composition of *Zarathustra* in ways that suggest a completely spontaneous process—*wie aus einem Guss*, as the Germans say—where all critical faculties were suspended: "If you have even the slightest residue of superstition, you will hardly reject the idea of someone being just an incarnation, mouthpiece, or medium of overpowering forces. The idea of revelation in the sense of something suddenly becoming *visible* and audible with unspeakable assurance and subtlety, something that throws you down and leaves you deeply shaken—this simply describes the facts of the case. You listen, you do not look for anything, you take, you do not ask who is there; a thought lights up in a flash, with necessity, without hesitation as to its form, — I never had any choice." (EH, Za 3). This account may or may not be accurate. But it doesn't preclude the likelihood that Nietzsche, *after* his "divine inspiration," carefully constructed, layered and edited the text.

Zarathustra's Introduction of the Overman

The overman makes his first appearance early on, in the Prologue to *Zarathustra*. It is the lengthiest and most sustained presentation of the metaphor both in the book and in his entire work. Therefore, it is crucial to look at how Zarathustra presents the metaphor here and what role it plays within the narrative progression of the Prologue.

An uncritical perspective, one that views Zarathustra's prophetic mission to proclaim the overman to be the central premise of the text, would take his message to the marketplace at face value. That is, Zarathustra, descending from the mountaintop to spread his new-found wisdom to the people, comes to herald *the* insight of the text, one that will help mankind supersede what Zarathustra calls the "Last Man." Indeed, it is the existence and prevalence of the Last Man, the conceptual foil to the overman, which makes the overman a metaphoric signpost toward which man should strive. The Last Man and the overman represent two sides of the same coin, the one necessitating the other.

Looking more closely at how Nietzsche presents the overman, it is clear that Zarathustra speaks in a language that echoes the evolutionary progressivism that late nineteenth European culture had assimilated in the twenty-five years since Darwin's *Origin of Species* had been published (*Origin* in 1859, *Zarathustra* in 1883-85).[6] Nowhere in Europe was Darwin's theory of evolution as widely, uncritically and wholeheartedly accepted as in Germany. Speaking to the marketplace, Zarathustra presents, with evolutionary cadences, the overman as a bridge to a higher human in the same way that the ape must now appear an embarrassing forbear to the modern human.

Thus Zarathustra conveys the sense of an overman that is a *willed* overcoming of the "human, all-too-human" Last Man, who revels in his mediocrity and who would represent a shameful precursor to a future overman. It is insignificant whether Nietzsche "gets Darwin wrong" here,[7] i.e., whether he adopts a form of teleological progressivism in his awareness of the overman that Darwin never espoused in his scientific notion of evolution. What is relevant is that Zarathustra himself chooses to present the overman in just such terms, because it is the only way that contemporary man, the man on the marketplace,

---

[6] For a full-length study of Nietzsche's engagement with Darwin's theories, see Dirk R. Johnson, *Nietzsche's Anti-Darwinism* (Cambridge: Cambridge University Press, 2010).

[7] "Nietzsche's criticisms and amendments are wrong not about Darwin, but about the facts, as we now know them; on these points Darwin has been confirmed, and Nietzsche's doubts no weight" (John Richardson, *Nietzsche's New Darwinism*. New York: Oxford University Press, 2004), 17.

can comprehend and register Zarathustra's message. In a culture saturated by Darwin's theories, Zarathustra's words must be mediated through the prism of that paradigm or else it could not connect with the masses.

The nineteenth-century evolutionary paradigm, therefore, is one part of the cultural backdrop to the text, but it also a cultural awareness that Nietzsche both incorporates and subverts at the same time. The subtlety of the text is that Zarathustra himself is unaware of the fragility of his position at the outset and must be made aware of it through experiences on his subsequent journey.

Zarathustra cannot therefore just be the innocent mouthpiece of this new awareness, since he is an extension of Nietzsche's larger narrative objective—to show how Zarathustra still carries in him the resentment that he wishes to overcome. The notion of the overman is still informed by the evolutionary idealism of the age, as is Zarathustra, who at this point does not mean to challenge the paradigm but to infuse it with his "higher" content. A culture that has absorbed the evolutionary paradigm can only conceive of an overman that is an idiosyncratic version of some "higher" human type.

But already by the second half of the Prologue, Nietzsche distances Zarathustra from the position he first articulated in the marketplace. With the dramatic death of the socially maligned tightrope walker, who now becomes the most promising possibility for a higher human type, Zarathustra reassesses his original objective. The tightrope walk of course echoes back to Zarathustra's earlier image of the bridge that connects man to overman. But here, the tightrope walker falls to his death on his way across the span, not reaching the other side. Zarathustra now regards this figure as the better material from which to fashion the overman.

Nietzsche, at this point, does not give up on the overman as such, but changes who should become the carrier of the ideal: a man like the tightrope walker, who, with courage and humility, "does his job." By the end of the Prologue, Zarathustra has not yet given up on the ideal itself, only shifted its focus. And finally, in the closing sections of the Prologue, he declares that solitary individuals will become the recipients of his message, no longer the masses. These individuals have a better chance of carrying the seed for the overman.

Thus, in the short span of the Prologue's ten sections, Nietzsche has performed a crucial pivot, thereby problematizing Zarathustra's mission. The overman was at first resoundingly declared the objective for mankind, and the central metaphor was etched in the readers' imagination. But going forward, the overman loses its contours, gets filled with different contents along the way, but never again assumes concrete shape. The metaphor of the overman compares to what Nietzsche famously described as truths no longer believed in but that continue on as metaphors: "coins which have lost their pictures and now matter only as metal, no longer as coins" (*On Truth and Lie in an Extra-Moral Sense*, 1873).

Nietzsche's Understanding of Man

The highly influential early text *On Truth and Lie in an Extra-Moral Sense* is also the place to start with an examination into Nietzsche's understanding of man. A current line of reading has it that the ideas Nietzsche presents in this text, above all his skepticism toward the possibility of truth, would be rebuked in the late texts, where Nietzsche would return to a position consonant with (scientific) truth.[8] But this perspective is highly suspect. On the contrary, the ideas expressed in this text are the fertile seedbed out of which the rest of his philosophy grew. His later insights would be more sophisticated and wide-ranging chords from this original score.

One of the key insights Nietzsche challenges here, radical for the time, though highly cogent in its line of argumentation, is our faith in fixed linguistic concepts. Nietzsche explains the impossibility of defining a unique type, a conceptual signpost, under which one can subsume the multifarious individuations of nature. All attempts to do so reflected an anthropomorphism through which man tried to explain, and thereby master, the essential inscrutability, randomness and chaos of nature. Here, Nietzsche already exhibits a decidedly anti-Platonic animus. But curiously, Nietzsche also uses the word *Gattung* with which Germans designated Darwinian "species". Implicitly, Nietzsche already questions the basic building block of Darwinian theory; he doubts the existence of fixed forms and suggests, instead, that surface similarity is a cover for endless variation:

> We obtain the concept, as we do the form, by overlooking what is individual and actual; whereas nature is acquainted with no forms and no concepts, and likewise with no species [*Gattung*], but only with an X which remains inaccessible and undefinable for us. For even our contrast between individual and species is something anthropomorphic and does not originate in the essence of things.

---

[8] Maudemarie Clark argues this position in *Nietzsche on Truth and Philosophy*. Cambridge: Cambridge UP, 1990.

Instead of "species," or *Gattung*, we should learn to discern and to appreciate the nuances that are concealed by conceptual simplification.

In the texts that follow in the so-called middle period, and until *Zarathustra*, Nietzsche expanded on this premise and examined the human type—however, not based not on its communalities, i.e., that which fixed the human as a distinct species type, but rather on the differences. From various angles, he argued that the "self" is a conceptual myth, by which man tried to fashion a firm identity out of a storehouse of conflicting drives and instincts. Man's inner life, like nature itself, was in constant flux, which led individuals to simplify the reality of their inner life—and the interpretation of the natural world—for the sake of survival. As he already noted in the earlier text: unbeknown to man, and at the most subconscious level, conflicting drives were creating false impressions and vast simplifications that deluded him into believing in the fixity of self, forms and nature itself.

We can now return to the notion of the overman. If the above is Nietzsche's basic insight in relation to man—one which did not change but only deepened over time—then the overman for him could not represent a higher human type, because he doubted a higher "type" could be fixed or that such a "type" existed at all. There could only be individual humans—better, individuations—randomly emerging within the constant flux of nature. That higher type could also not have fixed qualities that would allow it to serve as an ideal for mankind; it could only reveal itself and take on identity in the process—in an active and direct engagement with the outside world.

Only in retrospect might a "superior" individual incite our admiration and wonder, for it will have revealed a harmonious coordination of the instincts that held out a promise for future individuals. In short, the overman as a "higher" human type could not serve as any goal or objective for a future humanity, because such an "ideal" toward which one could systematically work didn't exist. There was no blueprint, no master plan; a "higher" human just emerged—at random, unexpected and unplanned. An idealized higher human, in the way Nietzsche envisioned it, could not be willed into existence, nor could mankind work toward it.

Let us examine a couple of passages to determine this. One of the most crucial in this regard lies on the other spectrum of Nietzsche's philosophical development: one of two late "Anti-Darwin" passages (1888) in his notebooks. Here Nietzsche talks about the figure of Caesar as a consummate higher human being:

> The richest and most complex forms—for nothing more is meant by the term 'higher type'—perish more easily: only lower forms hold fast to an apparent immutability. […] In mankind, too, under ever-fluctuating favorable and unfavorable conditions, higher types, the lucky strikes of development, perish more easily. […] The short lifespan of beauty, of genius, of a Caesar, such a type does not get passed down. The type gets passed down; a type is nothing extreme, not a lucky strike (KSA 13, 317).

The generic "type," in Nietzsche's understanding, is the "apparent" average individual, the run-of-the middle human, whose will is always in danger of degenerating and who thus seeks to create a permanent dam against instinctual decline. The "type" is "apparent" and seems fixed [*scheinbare Unvergänglichkeit*], because the will, through rituals, habits and consistent practices, can help sustain itself against internal decadence; these practices are its measures against decay, its mask to conceal instinctual decline. While such individuals succeed in creating a temporary type, a deceptive permanence within flux, it is one that arises through a violent, cruel subjugation of the inner life (see GM II, 17).

In relation to the overman, the crucial point is the contrast: the lucky strike, the Caesar. Nietzsche suggests here that the higher type is neither planned, nor can it be passed down. Rather than seek methods to combat decadence, the superior will *instinctively* picks the right remedies and orders its instinctual chaos.[9] But *that* individual will cannot be (genetically) passed down,[10] precisely because it is *not* fixed, nor does it want to be; it embraces chaos and flux, and it masters the impermanency and turbulence that both nature and the inner life constantly present. That is what makes it a higher type—a being that is reflective, at a higher level of coordination, of nature itself. If such a higher type triumphs, it

---

[9] Nietzsche summarizes all the requirements that a "higher type" will have in the term *Wohlgerathenheit* ("state of being well-turned out") (EH, Wise 2). With this term, Nietzsche emphasizes qualities that reflect instinctual accuracy in making the right choices for one's personal well-being. A higher type is higher simply because he is, and that is reflected in his choices and the decisions he makes.

[10] The discovery of Mendel's Law, and the subsequent science of genetics, occurred after Nietzsche's productive career. But this is irrelevant for Nietzsche's insights. The science of modern genetics is focused on fixed biological traits that get genetically passed down, thus suggesting a fatalistic determinacy in our characters and behavior. But Nietzsche seems to suggest, instead, that what gets passed down (genetically) is only one contributing factor and not alone decisive. It is how one coordinates and psychically deals with (genetic) inheritance that determines human potential.

can only be due to a lucky coincidence, a fortunate constellation of events; most times higher types perish.

In one of the rare passages in the late published texts, post *Zarathustra*, where Nietzsche refers to an overman, in *Antichrist* 4 (1888), he writes (in the same year as the above):

> in another sense, there is a continuous series of individual successes in the most varied places on earth and from the most varied cultures; here, a *higher type* does in fact present itself, a type of overman in relation to humanity. Successes like this, real strokes of luck, were always possible and perhaps will always be possible.

The word overman here is used not in a future-directed sense, but as a point of contrast and distinction, as an example of an exceptional type, in order to distinguish it from the wide swath of humanity (similar in function to the Last Man in the Prologue).[11] In hindsight, certain individuals, certain peoples will seem higher, because they exhibit a superior instinctual coordination and can appear to us, from our current vantage point, as "real strokes of luck" [*Glücksfälle*]. Nietzsche uses the metaphor in deliberately qualifying terms ("a *type* of overman"). There is no indication as to which particular character traits or features distinguish such a higher type or how, or even *if*, such a type will be possible again in the future ("*perhaps* will always be possible").

Finally, a couple of important references appear in Nietzsche's treatment of *Zarathustra* in his retrospective account, *Ecce Homo* (1888). These are especially important, because they refer back to the prime text in which the metaphor appears and hint further at how he wishes the overman to be understood. (Another important passage in this regard is his famous example of Cesare Borgia as a better example of the overman than Parsifal [EH, Books 1], though I will not examine it here.) In the first example, Nietzsche speaks of

> the ideal of a spirit who plays naively, i.e. not deliberately but from an overflowing abundance and power, with everything that was hitherto called holy, good, untouchable, divine [...]; the ideal of a human, superhuman well-being and benevolence that will often enough appear inhuman—for example,

---

[11] Nietzsche, when writing *about* the overman, uses it as a *comparative* term; it is superhuman *not* in *absolute* terms, but only in contradistinction to the current human type: "[Zarathustra] does not conceal the fact that *his* type of person—a type that is an overman in comparison—is an overman specifically when compared to the good, that the good and just would call his overmen *devils*."(EH, Destiny 5).

when it places itself next to all earthly seriousness heretofore, all forms of solemnity in gesture, word, tone, look, morality, and task as if it were their most incarnate and involuntary parody—and in spite of all this, it is perhaps only with it that the great seriousness really emerges (EH, Za 2).

In the second example, Nietzsche claims that the figure of Zarathustra comes to embody the "ideal" through his actions and comportment—above all, in his engagement with others:

> And how Zarathustra descends and says the most gracious things to everybody! How gently he handles even his adversaries, the priests, and suffers with them and from them! – At every moment here, humanity has been overcome, the idea of "overman" has become the highest reality, – everything that was considered great about people lies infinitely far *beneath* him (EH, Za 6).

In both examples, Nietzsche suggests that the overman no longer signifies a future objective, as he did for Zarathustra at the outset, but is realized in the comportment of Zarathustra on his journey. Zarathustra himself models *through* his actions and bearing a higher type, which he had at first posited as ideal for everyone. The adjectival form of the noun, combined with the "human" [*menschlich-übermenschlichen*], indicates that its qualities refer to actions—i.e., to an inner spontaneous affirmative energy directed outward ("from an overflowing abundance and power")—and are not bound to a fixed type. And it indicates that the *being* overhuman (his actual reality, not as a form of future transcendence) is realized in the *doing*, in the actions themselves. It expends itself, is actuated, in *action*, in particular, in the way Zarathustra interacts with his instinctual opposites and adversaries—even with those who would call him "inhuman." Finally, by becoming an example of such an overman, Zarathustra has left "humanity" beneath him, both in concrete terms as well as a term to designate a common human goal.

But what has transpired? How did Zarathustra himself become "the ideal" that he promulgates and why does the overman as an ideal for everyone recede by the end of the text?

Zarathustra's Encounter with the Eternal Return

We must here put the metaphor of the overman on ice and see what occurs in the narrative after Zarathustra announces he will seek "solitary individuals." As indicated, Zarathustra hadn't given up on the overman; he had only redirected his message to a new target audience. In the following two parts, Zarathustra no longer refers much to the overman, but instead sounds out individuals on his journey and declares his aversion and disgust with his age. In Part I, he gives various speeches where he rejects contemporary culture and warns his followers not to be seduced by the false ideals and values of the present. At this stage, the overman remains an undercurrent: the hidden context and signpost for a possible future overcoming of the sickening present.

But an increasingly melancholy and introspective mood grips Zarathustra in Part II (e.g., see "The Grave Song" and the "Dance Song") and there are signs of a momentous event to come: the thought of the eternal return. In the final section of Part II, "The Stillest Hour," a voice tells Zarathustra that he hasn't found the courage to face his most hidden thought, and in the first major section in the following Part III, "The Vision and the Riddle," Zarathustra delivers his first *mediated* experience with the eternal return: he tells seafarers on a journey, in the form of a riddle, the story of a shepherd choking with a snake stuck in his throat. On his journey until now, Nietzsche implies, Zarathustra has shied away from this ultimate awareness but he can no longer avoid a confrontation with it.

The most extensive exposition of the eternal return occurs in one of the concluding sections of Part III, "The Convalescent." Only now is Zarathustra in the position to confront the thought. For such a significant metaphor, perhaps more significant in the reception than the overman, Nietzsche says very little about the eternal return in concrete terms. But as I have stated about the overman, the metaphors in this text have taken on a life of their own and have rarely been analyzed in terms of their function.

What Zarathustra describes in his ultimate encounter with the thought, which he calls up from his depths, is not a fundamental cosmological principle, nor a teaching about how the world actually *is*, but how Zarathustra now recognizes it to be. Zarathustra is confronted with the "horrible" *thought* that all things recur, the greatest and the smallest, and that the greatest, too, are frightfully small. This awareness fills him with crippling disgust. When his animals seek to make a hurdy-gurdy song from this "world-defining thought," the Eternal Return, Zarathustra retreats in silence. As a projection of his subjective state, his innermost being, the thought cannot become a metaphor for all.

Of course, the repercussion of the awareness is that the overman, as previously conceived, must fall victim to this thought. There are two reasons for this. For one, Zarathustra's bitterness and disappointment with his age was the hidden reservoir for the thought of the overman in the first place: namely, it was his revulsion with the "good" that "gave him wings to 'glide off into distant futures'" (EH, Destiny 5). Zarathustra's latent disgust with life and his residual pity with man, reinforced by his self-imposed solitude on the mountaintop, engendered a visionary future ideal type that reflected the conceptual opposite of current man, the Last Man. Similar to all prophets who flee the world, Zarathustra had fashioned a counter-ideal from the hurt and bitterness he felt with *this* world.

But the deep animus Zarathustra harbors against his age was coaxed out of him, and he was forced to confront the realization that there could never be an escape from this world. There could be no better, higher or transcendent, only the dross of the human in all perpetuity. The overman, too, in other words, represents an escape from the horror of the all-too-human present into the comfort of a future ideal. Resentment—unacknowledged and deeply submerged at first, but now rising from psychic depths to the surface—had been the seedbed for the thought of an overman.

Secondly, and this refers back to what I said about his scientific understanding of man, there could be no "over" to the present. The recognition of the perpetual ebb and flow of the moment, with the high and low forever mixing, as expressed in Zarathustra's words of disgust, meant that there could never be a fixed type that could transcend and hold itself. As Nietzsche wrote in scientific terms in response to Darwin: "The entire animal and plant world does not evolve from higher to lower…. Rather, everything at the same time, one on top of another, pell-mell, and in strife [*übereinander und durcheinander und gegeneinander*]" (KSA 13, 317).

Nietzsche suggests a new awareness. A "higher type" no longer seeks refuge in an ideal, but can affirm and embrace the eternal return of the same and accept its life, as is, for all eternity. It could immerse itself into *this* world, accept and master life in its complexity, and stamp its affirmation on the always-present moment. The affirmation of the eternal return without resentment becomes the hallmark of a higher type. This type,

> "conceives of reality *as it is*: his type has the strength to do this—, it is not alienated, removed from reality, it is *reality itself*, it contains in itself everything terrible and questionable about reality, *this is the only way someone can achieve greatness…*" (EH Destiny 5).

The overman as an ideal for all mankind had been rendered superfluous. Zarathustra, incorporating the eternal return, had himself become the higher type that he had at first prophesized for all. There was no longer the overman; there was only the "human, overhuman" benevolence of Zarathustra.

Conclusion

In comparison to his other texts, *Zarathustra* appears to stand alone—self-contained and timeless. At least Nietzsche seems to want us to think so. In *Ecce Homo*, he writes in hyperbolic terms:

> This work stands entirely on its own. Leaving aside the poets: perhaps nothing has ever been done with such an excess of energy. Here, my concept of the "Dionysian" became the highest deed; all the rest of human activity looks poor and limited in comparison. [...] Wisdom, investigations of the soul, the art of speaking—none of this existed before Zarathustra (EH, Za 6).

Nietzsche furthers this impression by choosing Zarathustra, an ancient Persian prophet, to be his messenger. According to Nietzsche, "Zarathustra *created* this fateful error of morality: this means he must be the first to *recognize* it" (EH, Destiny 3). One of the jarring features of the text, its very strangeness, is the bizarre incongruity of a little-known historical prophet being thrust into a contemporary European setting. In addition, Nietzsche's work exhibits numerous archaizing features—Biblical cadences and oracular pronouncements—which suggest that he naively donned the garb of a prophet to proclaim new truths (the Overman, the Eternal Return) to a world disrupted by the "death of God." However, these superficial features conceal and distract from narrative strategies that Nietzsche intentionally built into the work but that often get overlooked in critical response to it.

For one, despite the fact that Nietzsche modeled Zarathustra on a legendary figure, who embodies many archaic attributes, his Zarathustra represents a fully *modern* individual, one who wrestles with, and lives out, all the tensions, disruptions and mindsets of his time—late nineteenth-century European civilization. Nietzsche's age is fully incorporated into the text. It is not only its backdrop and the target of many of Zarathustra's barbs; it receives the brunt of his antipathy, wrath and frustration. It is what he must overcome in himself and, above all, what *we* as readers must overcome in *ourselves* if we are to discern and appreciate the depth of his critique.

One of the prime examples is the metaphor of the overman. Coming down from his secluded mountaintop, Zarathustra presents the overman at the beginning of the Prologue as a response to the nihilism of his age, as a guidepost for a future humanity that can redeem the present. Most readers have taken this to be a straightforward injunction: "The overman is the meaning of the earth" (Za, Prologue 3)! Yet, they forget that Zarathustra, before he is introduced, had left society and sought isolation out of his discontent with the present—the standard practice of prophets.

The solution that Zarathustra presents to the marketplace upon his return to society, the overman, originates from his despair with the present. And above all, Zarathustra couches the ideal in terms that still show the vestiges of his age: he introduces it as an idealized form of higher humanity. The spirit of Darwin and evolution, which had engulfed his age, *similarly* informs Zarathustra's response to the present. As a child of his time, Zarathustra affirms a form of idealism that seeks a future ideal in order to escape disgust with his contemporaries.

But as Zarathustra comes to realize during his journey and encounters, above all, in his experience with the eternal return, is that his latent resentment, his anger with his past (see "The Grave Song") and with the absurdity of the present ("The Convalescent"), had taken hold of him at a root level and had propelled him on his mission. The fantasy of an evolutionary progression to a higher being, to a humanity that could transcend the present, was just another facet of the accursed ideal, an escape from reality. That reality, Zarathustra discovers, is reflected in the eternal return. The absurdity and nihilism of the present, he now recognizes, cannot be transcended or overcome; on the contrary, their eternal return had to be recognized, accepted, and even affirmed.

An overman, therefore, could not represent an overcoming of the present in some future humanity; instead, a superhuman type needs to master the ever-present moment, by affirming itself, and life, in a continuous confrontation with the age—by *self*-overcoming. That challenge could not be met by fleeing from reality—as Zarathustra chose for himself, at first, by retreating to the solitude of the mountaintop. It could only be met by a full immersion into life and by exhibiting benevolence even towards those who continuously threaten to evoke his pity (see *Zarathustra*, Part IV). The figure of Zarathustra starts by evading reality and ends by embracing it.

Recognizing these narrative strategies, seeing how Nietzsche implicates Zarathustra in his critique of the age, will help cure us from falling for his suggestive metaphors. For generations of readers, the central metaphors in *Zarathustra* have been taken at face value and as core constituents of Nietzsche's philosophy. It is now time to challenge that perspective and to suggest a reading that examines the function and role of those metaphors in the highly sophisticated narrative that is *Zarathustra*.

Works Cited

The quotations from *Ecce Homo*, the *Antichrist* and *Zarathustra* come from the following editions:

Ecce Homo, translated by Judith Norman (Cambridge: Cambridge University Press, 2005)

The Antichrist, translated by Judith Norman (Cambridge: Cambridge University Press, 2005)

Thus Spoke Zarathustra, translated by Adrian del Caro (Cambridge: Cambridge University Press, 2006)

All other translations are the author's own.

Body-perspective or the Meaning of Subject in Nietzsche's Zarathustra

Thaís Helena Smilgys[1]

> But to them it is a sickly thing, and gladly would they jump out of their skin. Hence they listen to the preachers of death and they preach of hinterworlds themselves. Hear my brothers, hear the voice of the healthy body: a more honest and purer voice is this. More honestly and more purely speaks the healthy body, the perfect and perpendicular body, and it speaks of the meaning of the earth. (Z: 1 "On the Afterworldly)

This article addresses the question of the meaning of the body (*Leib*) that appears in the Zarathustra and in what way can we relate it to the idea of perspectivism. That is, it seeks to explore the relationship between body and perspective insofar as it constitutes the very idea of subject.

The essential thesis which will be explored is not that there are worlds as well as points of view, but that these worlds are real - or better – these worlds are a reality because they correspond to a specific body. This seemingly extraordinary statement means that the subject creates what he "sees" through the body (Viveiros de Castro, 2014).

This image of the cosmos, in which the bodies are regarded as great differentiators, also posits the fundamental transformability of the cosmos: metamorphoses between species are a natural condition. Metamorphosis is not only the usual declaration of origin in myth, it is still possible in today's life. In this sense, perspectivism is the ability to occupy a point of view. The "other" of the subject is not an object, but another subject; and subjectivation is exactly what perspectivism describes.

In Nietzsche's Zarathustra this idea appears clearly: "*like me, the virtue that has flown back to earth - yes, back to life and body (Leib): that it gives the earth its meaning, a human sense!*"[2]. Jean-Luc Nancy also explains in other words: "*nothing escapes from the subject, it governs the world (...) the Subject is the ultimate ground or subiectum on the*

---

[1] PhD in Philosophy and General Theory of Law at the University of São Paulo, Brazil (2015-2018), with a research internship at the Universität Stuttgart, Germany (2017), with supervision of Prof. Dr. Claus Zittel. thsmilgys@gmail.com or smilgys@usp.br
[2] *Zarathustra*, I, 2. „*führt, gleich mir, die verflogene Tugend zur Erde zurück — ja, zurück zu Leib und Leben: dass sie der Erde ihren Sinn gebe, einen Menschen-Sinn!*"

basis of which can be know, calculated, mastered and exploited[3] , This means that it is only from the perspective of the subject that we can conceive the world. More precisely, we only know the world through the subject that remains in a specific body.

In this sense, the cognitively interesting process in Zarathustra, as Viveiros de Castro (2014) identifies in Amerindian Perspectivism, is one that we can find "l'ordre des raisons", that is, "the human finger" in the cosmos. The fact is that this "ideal of subjectivity" opens up the possibility of understanding certain "phenomena" that could not be understood by the "ideal of objectivity" and will be the thesis of this paper.

It is clear to notice that Nietzsche sees that our perception depends on our perspective and in turn on our body. By body, he means not physiological differences, but capacities and dispositions that make the body of each species unique: what is eaten, what is communicated, where it lives, whether it is a gregarious species, that is, a herd animal, or a species whose relatives prefer to roam alone. It is not about the body as a fixed form, but as an assemblage of affects that constitute a *habitus*.

Therefore, the idea that arises can be delimited in the following way: the body as placed by Zarathustra is not only the criticism to the concept of superiority of the soul elaborated in the metaphysical tradition as the condition of possibility of knowledge but the possibility to return the man as a perspective like any creature in the world.

With Nietzsche and from his idea of the subject as creation is presented the material relationship of this man with the body as a field of experimentation on which the effect of power creates the subject. It is precisely at this point that the problematic of the subject attached to the body reveals the conditions of possibility which, if taken as a space of subjectivation, are the propelling mechanism of a metaphysics that, at the same time, can found the subject and the society. In the sayings of Zarathustra the problematic is revealed:

---

[3] In this context, the importance of Nancy's work lies in the way it allows us to think of the perhaps inevitable persistence of the subject, not as the persistence of a metaphysical substance or ground, but as an instance which is constantly ungrounded and exposed to unmasterable excess. This instance would be temporalizing, singular and plural giving of being itself which would be irreducible to any concept or figure and any possibility of ontological disclosure. Subject occupies an uncertain place at the limit of representation. It figures an unfigurable instance and as such internalizes a difference with itself. Ian James: *Jean-Luc Nancy – The Persistence of the Subject.* in: *Paragraph.* Vol. 25, No. 1, Edinburgh University Press, 2002, S. 125-141.

> Thus the body goes through history, becoming and fighting. And the spirit – what is it to the body? The herald of its fights and victories, companion and echo. Parables are all names of good and evil: they do not express, they only hint. A fool who wants to know of them! Pay attention, my brothers, to every hour where your spirit wants to speak in parables: there is the origin of your virtue. There your body is elevated and resurrected; with its bliss it delights the spirit, which becomes creator and esteemer and lover and benefactor of all things. (Z: 1 "On the Gift-Giving Virtue)

At last, man finds a way to escape from himself, exerting against his body the most brutal of violence. Violence that removes from life any meaning other than those authorized by Reason and, under this structure, also delegates to this Reason all authority for the exercise of the drive according to a legality external to life. Here is the man, in this violent rupture with the "Hericlitean flow" of life, fixed for the first time in his truculent intellectual sovereignty.

The product of this rationality, as well as of those that followed, would be the "bad conscience": that it is born as this disease that inhibits the discharge out of feelings and instincts, selecting as legitimate intermediary all corporeal life, that is:

> It was the sick and the dying-out who despised the body and the earth and invented the heavenly and its redeeming drops of blood. But even these sweet and shadowy poisons they took from the body and the earth! They wanted to escape their misery and the stars were too distant for them. So they sighed "Oh if only there were heavenly paths on which to sneak into another being and happiness!" – Then they invented their schemes and bloody little drinks! Now they fancied themselves detached from this earth, these ingrates. But what did they have to thank for the fits and bliss of their detachment? Their body and this earth. (Z: 1 "On the Afterworldly)

Thus, in criticizing this disgust for the body, Zarathustra is able to make the body the *"embrayeur"* that allows the passage of the material field to the supernatural and is itself the perspective of the creatures that inhabit the world and in this sense the body becomes the perspective (the more different bodies that exist, the more perspectives are possible). Thus, it does not correspond to a pure and simple inversion, but to a re-elaboration of the idea of the body.

This re-appropriation of body/soul duality as the founding mechanism of the subject is taken by Werner Stegmaier (2015) as the prime articulation of the possibilities of perspectives, that is, of the possibilities of seeing in each movement of subjectivation a movement of otherness, according to which homogenizing adjunction of metaphysics does not allow us to glimpse the constant disjunction of the "subjectable" elements, thus producing, constantly, perspectives, that is, for him:

> Conceived of without transcendental *a prioris*, the subject becomes a mere individual, which is different from any other individual and which in its own subjectivity cannot reach the subjectivity of another subject. Subjects remain separated, no matter how much they manage to desubjectivize themselves. They are, in a word, perspectives. (Stegmaier, 494)

With Nietzsche's Zarathustra it is possible to rethink the relation of knowledge, precisely under the conception of the subject as perspective, that is, as a proposal of a disjunctive synthesis to think the "humanity of humanity". This movement opens, therefore, the possibility of conceiving a form of knowledge that is not objectification, but subjectivation and personification in which *"multinaturalism affirms not so much a variety of natures as the naturalness of variation-variation as nature"*(Viveiros De Castro, 74)

It is then a matter of varying the plurality of bodies and the variation of meanings adjacent to them according to the most varied possibilities of variations of meanings that each of them constructs and emits for themselves and for the others that relate to them. By such a way, as Nietzsche does in his Zarathustra, construct a philosophy of perspectives, in which ontology becomes properly an ontology of the inquiry of bodies and their possibilities of creation of senses (the donkey, the eagle, the panther, the snake, the mole, etc.). As Viveiros de Castro explains:

> I will re-emphasize it: such an anthropology would make multiplicities proliferate. Because it is not at all a question, as Derrida opportunely recalled (2008), of preaching the abolition of the borders that unite/separate sign and world, persons and things, "us" and "them," "humans" and "nonhumans"-easy reductionisms and mobile monisms are as out of the question as fusional fantasies- but rather of "unreducing" [irreduire] (Latour) and undefining them, by bending every line of division into an infinitely complex curve. It is not a question of erasing the contours but of folding and thickening them, diffracting and rendering them iridescent. "This is what we are getting at: a generalized chromaticism" (D. G. 1 987).(Viveiros De Castro, 45)

Thus, through the anthropological-philosophical view of Viveiros de Castro (2014) - and, likewise, in that of Stegmaier (2015), when comparing Luhmann's sociological subjectivation with that of Nietzsche - a questioning structure that removes the subject from its conditions "a priori" and allocates it in its historical-critical condition of articulation, among many and infinite others, of things and senses. By doing so, the "man" - especially the Western man, sublimely formulated from the philosophy of the subject - of his position of supremacy,

> Humanity is in the position of the common denominator, the reflexive mode of the collective, and is as such derived in relation to the primary positions of predator and prey, which necessarily implicates other collectives and personal multiplicities in a situation of perspectival multiplicity. This interspecific resemblance or kinship arises from the deliberate, socially produced suspension of a given predatory difference and does not precede it. (Viveiros De Castro, 45)

This possibility of seeing from bodies and multiples from it ceaselessly produced allows Zarathustra to walk among animals, kings, popes and from them capture their perspectives, their modes of subjectification, their regimes of creation in the senses, the forces that constitute them, the structures which, as an "a posteriori", construct from the corporeal regimes and the corporeal regimes. It allows, in short, new experiences on the one's own thought.

To think thus, a theory of knowledge by the body-to construct the Self-opens space for an idea of differential value of things and beings, that is, "a potential difference" that can be apprehended at the moment when the subject sees himself as the self in other species. That is, the "disappearance" of the bound subject indicates the edge of the self based on which it subsists, or to say as Jean-Luc Nancy, the subject's ground (*subiectum*) only appears as it simultaneously disappears and is able to place a punctual identity without identity, that exists in the spasm that articulates and dismembers the subject. All that resides after this moment of identity (*identité ponctuelle*) is only conceived as a mask, falsification, or imagination of itself as a fable.

Zarathustra's fables of the various bodies that inhabit the world, the eagle, the serpent, the donkey, are above all perspectives, that is, the essential thesis would not be so much that there are so many worlds as points of view, that these worlds are real, or more exactly are reality. The seemingly extraordinary postulate that each point of view defines a different world translates into the simple experience that each subject acts in function of what he sees and thereby realizes what he sees:

> Whence the regime of qualitative multiplicity proper to myth: the question, for example, of whether the mythic jaguar is a block of human affects having the form of a jaguar or a block of human affects having a human form is strictly undecidable, as mythic "metamorphosis" is an event, a change on the spot: an intensive superposition of heterogeneous states rather than an extensive transposition of homogenous states. Myth is not history because metamorphosis is not a process, was not yet a process and will never be a

> process. Metamorphosis is both anterior and external to the process of process-it is a figure (a figuration) of becoming. (Viveiros De Castro, 66)

In this sense, perspectivism is the capacity to occupy a point of view, as Zarathustra, the "non-human" occupies a point of view of the human - spatial and not mental - and, in this sense, could manifest a higher intensity to the human, in which would update the capability more fully. The perspectivism exposed by Nietzsche poses the question of the position of the subject not a mere logical possibility, but ontological potentiality. Perspectivism is, then, to say an epistemology with ontology[4], postulates this redistribution of unity and variation; in general, postulates only that reality is made up of subjects, of actors or, even more clearly, of authors with their worlds.

In addition, the idea of Nancy is retaken, it is observed that the author identifies this body doomed to combat and the relations of forces, it is not already the codified body, but this idea of a field, a space of subjectivation, *i.e.*,

> "Written bodies" -incised, engraved, tattooed, scarred-are precious bodies, preserved and protected like the codes for which they act as glorious engrams: but this isn't really the modern body, this isn't the body we've projected, there, ahead of us, approaching us, naked, merely naked, and *exscribed* in advance from all writing.(Nancy: Corpus, 11)

The essential problem is the body, to think the body and the subject in the body because it is *"a place that opens, displaces and spaces phallus and cephale: making room for them to create an event (rejoicing, suffering, thinking, being born, dying, sexing, laughing, sneezing, trembling, weeping, forgetting....)"*. (Nancy: Corpus, 17)

This idea of returning to the body as a condition of the possibility of knowledge (thus inverting the idea of modernity) reveals the problem of the body as capable of knowing. If in modernity there was a section between nature and society, Nietzsche, from the metaphors and fables of Zarathustra takes up this

---

[4] And to this ontological flattening corresponds a "symmetric" epistemology (Latour, 1993) rigorously put, we are witnessing the collapse of the distinction between epistemology (language) and ontology (world) and the progressive emergence of a "practical ontology" Oensen, 2004) in which knowing is no longer a way of repress: enting the unknown but of interacting with it, i.e., a way of creating rather than contemplating, reflecting, or communicating (see Deleuze and Guattari 1991). The task of knowledge is no longer to unify diversity through representation but, as Latour again puts it, of "multiplying the agents and agencies populating our world" (1996: 5). Viveiros De Castro, Eduardo, *Cannibal Metaphysics for a Post-Structural Anthropology*, (ed. and trasl. Skajish, Peter), Univocal, 2014, p. 105.

thought as a new conception of *socius* in that it is no longer conceived from the duality nature / culture or society / state. Or, as Derrida writes:

> Nietzsche's procedure (the generalization of metaphoricity by putting into *abyme* one determined metaphor) is possible only if one takes the risk of a continuity between the metaphor and the concept, as between animal and man, instinct and knowledge! In order not to wind up at an empiricist reduction of knowledge and a fantastic ideology of truth, one should surely substitute another articulation for the (maintained or erased) classical opposition of metaphor and concept. This new articulation, without importing all the metaphysics of the classical opposition, should also account for the specific divisions that epistemology cannot overlook, the divisions between what it calls metaphoric effects and scientific effects. The need for this new articulation has undoubtedly been called for by Nietzsche's discourse. It will have to provoke a displacement and an entire reinscription of the values of science and of truth, that is, of several others too. (Derrida, 262-3)

In sum, the analysis also seems to attract to *socius's* perspective Foucault's diagnosis of the uselessness, and even of the harm, caused by the theory of the subject to the human sciences: "man in itself" or "nature" would be pernicious premises, doomed to the overthrow[5].

Thus, if on the one hand the initial picture whose image that is placed is of the necessary and universal subject, an autonomous subject, that is, of the ethical totality of Kant, and thus guarantees to all scientific knowledge the uniformization of the answers, with Nietzsche and from his idea of the subject as creation is presented the material relation with the body, field of experimentation on which the effect of power creates the subject. That is, for the proposed thesis to enter into the horizon of the logical "purity" of things, it is necessarily to enter into the relation of forces that such technique impinges,

---

[5] And that appearance was not the liberation of an old anxiety, the transition into luminous consciousness of an age-old concern, the entry into objectivity of something that had long remained trapped within beliefs and philosophies: it was the effect of a change in the fundamental arrangements of knowledge. As the archaeology of our thought easily shows, man is an invention of recent date. And one perhaps nearing its end. If those arrangements were to disappear as they appeared, if some event of which we can at the moment do no more than sense the possibility – without knowing either what its form will be or what it promises–were to cause them to crumble, as the ground of Classical thought did, at the end of the eighteenth century, then one can certainly wager that man would be erased, like a face drawn in sand at the edge of the sea. Foucault, Michel, *The Order of Things: An Archaeology of the Human Sciences*, Routledge, 2004, p. 422.

79

corroborates, imputes[6]. It is, in addition, the deviation of the visibility of such forces, by a technique that never reaches its own force to the powerful individual.

In this reading the subject is the product of a social practice that permeates the history of subjectivity and consequently re-elaborates the idea of the body, since Zarathustra's perspective, and in this a-historical aspect (unrelated to the linear history of events) the origin of a subject, but its positivity; its creation in a normativity: the inscription of the body in the field of action of the individual.

Of course, the consequences of this remission are pertinent to the whole of this work, however, here one of them is essential. That is, the linkage of the subject's escape to the escape of the senses unified by subjectivation.[7] In this way, only by escaping the subject's trap, with its significant chains, is it possible to escape from its siege. After all, the task is to escape from the infinite capacity for unification of meanings operationalized by the subject and his vision.

It is, as Nancy would say, the observation of the fictitious life signified by the representation that establishes death as the regulation of man; it is thus the

---

[6] As perspective, the subject has no free, synoptic, and unlimited view over the world, no ideas of the world from a standpoint from above the world. It is rather limited in his view of the world by a standpoint and horizon within the world; it is only inside these limits, which include logical, ontological and linguistic "schemata" (cf. NL 1886–87, 5[22], KSA 12: 193f.), that the subject can ever relate to any objects. What a perspective finds in its limits is also a foothold, a foothold in its life and perspectivity. A perspective in Nietzsche's sense is a 'lively' subject. It can widen or straighten its horizon and displace its standpoint, and thereby adapt both its horizon and its standpoint to its current life situation. But it always remains bound to a standpoint and horizon, it cannot arbitrarily abandon them (therefore, there is also no danger of a relativism of arbitrariness). Nevertheless, it can–even if always only from its own perspective (and hence again paradoxically)–place itself in the perspectives of others, and in this way increase the amplitude of its possibilities of perception; objectivity becomes then conceivable as multiperspectivity (cf. GM III 12). Stegmaier, Werner. *Subjects as Temporal Clues to Orientation: Nietzsche and Luhmann on Subjectivity*. In Bartholomew Ryan, Maria Joao Mayer Branco & João Constancio (eds.), Nietzsche and the Problem of Subjectivity. De Gruyter, 2015, p. 494.

[7] Un engagement ou une invention de sens, l'«introduction d'un sens», comme disait Nietzsche, c'est l'ouverture d'un monde, du monde de quelqu'un (d'un «sujet», comme l'entendent les lacaniens), car quelqu'un, chaque un, fait monde pour autant qu'il est au monde. Il s'agit que « le sujet s'approprie son monde et le crée comme «« monde » en le rendant extérieur». Mais pour cela, quelqu'un doit avoir accès au monde. Un « sujet » ne peut faire monde – faire sens – s'il ne peut s'exposer au monde de tous les mondes monadiques, à la mondialité comme telle. Cet accès ne peut avoir lieu par la seule vérité. Il y faut un pas de plus - le pas hors de l'analyse, le pas de l'analyse elle-même hors d'elle-même. Nancy, Jean-Luc, Le *Sens du monde*, Paris: Galilée, 1993, p. 79/80.

method of observation of life by means of which life itself "*la méthode étend sa validité au cas où elle ne peut s'appliquer: la vision du sujet par lui-même, la vision de la vision. La spéculation est fictice: aussi ne s'expose-t-elle pas par miroirs, mais par portraits-qui sont des masques.*" It is in front of the "*loi de la vérité cartésienne, c'est la loi de la vision du sujet, la loi de l'évidence (de la 'lumière naturelle'), qui fait la certitude, la perspective*". The will that "*nous avons vu ce que c'était que voir la prunelle par dedans: c'est voir, tout court, et donc ne pas voir la vision, ou bien c'est voir l'œil mort dans lequel on regarde. Voir l'œil vivant, c'est toujours 'regarder par dehors'. Voir l'œil, c'est voir le masque—c'est toujours voir la figuration, criante de vérité (…), du trou*" (Nancy: Ego, 89).

With Zarathustra each species becomes a centre of consciousness, for it is in the body that perception resides. Briefly, if in the form of anthropocentric thought, the only correct way to know things is always in the form of the object, since only objects and not subjects are known, the world created by Zarathustra is moved by another ideal: it is a world in which every object is conceived as a potential subject (the donkey, the panther, the snake are endowed with the subject's vision), and the ideal knowledge is that which is capable of determining in the object its subjective part: its subject.

In this sense the ideal that is sought is the ideal of subjectivity and not of objectivity. Obviously each has its gains and losses. The fact is that this ideal of subjectivity opens the possibility of understanding certain "phenomena" that could not be understood with the ideal of objectivity. One of these phenomena is that Nietzsche conceives creatures as potential subjects, a completely socio-morphic universe, in which society is the basic *status* of existence.

Works Cited

Castro, Eduardo Batalha Viveiros de, and Peter Skafish. *Cannibal Metaphysics: for a Post-Structural Anthropology.* Univocal, 2014.

Derrida, Jacques, and Alan Bass. *Margins of Philosophy.* Univ. of Chicago Press, 2009.

Foucault, Michel. *The Order of Things Archaeology of the Human Sciences.* Routledge, 2005.

Nancy, Jean-Luc. *Corpus.* Fordham University Press, 2008.

Nancy, Jean-Luc. *Ego Sum.* Flammarion, 1979.

Nietzsche, Friedrich, and Adrian Del Caro. *Thus Spoke Zarathustra: A Book for All and None.* Univ. Press, 2015.

Stegmaier, Werner. "Subjects as Temporal Clues to Orientation: Nietzsche and Luhmann on Subjectivity." *Nietzsche and the Problem of Subjectivity,* by João Constancio et al., De Gruyter, 2017, p. 494.

Say "Yes!" to the Demon:
Amor Fati in the Eternal Hourglass

Jeffrey Lucas

"The greatest weight.—What, if some day or night a demon were to steal after you into your loneliest loneliness and say to you: "This life as you now live it and have lived it, you will have to live once more and innumerable times more; and there will be nothing new in it, but every pain and every joy and every thought and sigh and everything unutterably small or great in your life will have to return to you, all in the same succession and sequence—even this spider and this moonlight between the trees, and even this moment and I myself. The eternal hourglass of existence is turned upside down again and again, and you with it, speck of dust!"

Would you not throw yourself down and gnash your teeth and curse the demon who spoke thus? Or have you once experienced a tremendous moment when you would have answered him: "You are a god and never have I heard anything more divine." If this thought gained possession of you, it would change you as you are or perhaps crush you. The question in each and every thing, "Do you desire this once more and innumerable times more?" would lie upon your actions as the greatest weight. Or how well disposed would you have to become to yourself and to life to crave nothing more fervently than this ultimate eternal confirmation and seal?"[1]*- F. Nietzsche*

§. Introductory Exegesis

What Nietzsche believes, but does not express, is that man does not yet know how to say "Yes!"[2] The challenge is presented as though there might exist clearly defined, dichotomous camps, some naturally disposed to praise the demon and some predisposed to the attitude of resentment. This is not the case. The antithetic pair is a false pretense intended to impact the reader—a hallmark of Nietzschean style: hyperbole and perlocutionary-focused prose. There is merely one kind of listener the demon can find, who is invariably lacking whatever it is that constitutes yes-saying character: "even the greatest all-to-

---

[1] Nietzsche, Friedrich Wilhelm. *The Gay Science: With a Prelude in Rhymes and an Appendix of Songs.* Trans. Walter Kaufmann (New York: Vintage Books, 1974), 273. Aphorism: 341: *The Greatest Weight.*

[2] Disclaimer: for the sake of maintaining the Nietzschean vernacular, I will retain the use of the masculine third-person pronoun.

human." [3] The challenge, then, is also a *call* intended to destabilize, what Nietzsche perceives to be, our natural timidity, i.e., were we to confront the proclamation of the *eternal recurrence*. Just as man does not yet know how to re-absorb the theogonic responsibility of the *death of God*, and all the consequences necessarily entailed in such a meta-cosmic event, so too, he is equally unaware of the meaning and weight pertinent to a hypothetical affirmation of the demon's revelation. [4] This knowledge underlies the purpose of the aphorism, and, as though it were a tactical secret, Nietzsche remains silent on this point: he knows he is too early, and should not say too much if he is to affect the reader, like the early-ears of the villagers visited by Zarathustra. What we will soon realize is that the end of *amor fati* (as venerate praise of the demon) is not, itself, its fulfillment. We are not expected to literally become an *Übermensch*, as though saying "Yes!" to the demon were an easy feat; the moral of the parable is for *amor fati* to become the highest value in the eternal struggle of our own finitude. *It is in creating and implementing ever new possibilities of self-creation; a striving for aesthetic-autonomy and imagining how one might live in such a way as to become someone who might be predisposed to exclaim a hypothetical "Yes!"*

§I. Situated in Controversy

It is uniquely unavoidable with this (or any other) reading that we enter an ongoing controversy. Since the publication of Elizabeth-Forrester Nietzsche and Peter Gast's *The Will to Power*, the sense of the eternal recurrence has been re-framed to denote a metaphysical theory of cosmology. As a result, inconsistencies arise with the material published during Nietzsche's actual lifetime. The question of the eternal recurrence now becomes: does its sense reside in the hyperbolic parable or the propositional cosmology? (This is part of a larger problem that inhabits Nietzsche's work: how do we make sense of his early perspectivism in conjunction with his later metaphysics?) The propositional view confirms the criticism of Heidegger and others, who claim that Nietzsche was the *last metaphysician* and an *inverted Platonist*. Nearly every critic considers the significance of the parable to be a consequence of the eternal recurrence as a theoretical proposition; a transcendental ground of Becoming, or *the being of becoming*, as Deleuze postulates. A common interpretation we come across accounts for both senses in a one-way relation: *The Greatest Weight* aphorism expresses the moral component of a larger metaphysics outlined in

---

[3] Nietzsche, Friedrich Wilhelm. *Thus Spoke Zarathustra: A Book for All and None*. Trans. Walter Kaufmann (New York: Modern Library, 1995), 219.

[4] See *GS: The Madman*; aphorism *125*. Ibid. 181.

The Will to Power. But, in every case, the non-literal sense is made to cohere with its literal sense, and not vice versa. Might there be a means of expressing the metaphysical sense in terms of the moral-perlocutionary sense?

Such an argument would stand in contradistinction to Heidegger's view, that the first appearance is an underdeveloped "eccentricity," arbitrarily "tacked on"; a mere "playing with thoughts." [5] The eternal recurrence has a "shattering impact on all Being," he claims, but only in reference to its later, systematic formulation; anything shy of an articulation relevant to a *fundamental ontology* is superfluous (Ibid. 13). For Heidegger, this aphorism is a premature event. After all, Nietzsche did fail to follow through with his ten-year vow of silence (declared in a letter to Peter Gast), which only further supports Heidegger's derisive position—that Nietzsche's hastiness merely produced "cryptic passwords and parables" (14). The epiphany which brought about the *thought* (*Gedanke*[6]) of the eternal recurrence (August of 1881), and its first appearance less than a year later in the *Gay Science* (1882), both represent the infancy of the idea and a sterile incompleteness. I disagree in favor of the complete inverse; namely, that the *Grand Inspiration* in Sils Maria, and its first illustration (a poetic utterance), fully comprehends the scope of its meaning; these sites are not lacking in any way but, on the contrary, are totally encompassing of even the posthumous works.

The reading I propose emerges from an inextricable link between *amor fati*, as the greatest expression of the kind of *affirmation* the demon is attempting to spur in his listener, and the notion of *redemption*, introduced by Zarathustra, as the necessary condition of the former. To affirm a *now* is to affirm, as necessary, everything that preceded, and ultimately, gave birth to *this* moment in time. Rather than our past remaining a static regret or some contingent series of eventualities, we declare it to be a matter of our own will, retrospectively, from the point of view of a personal aesthetic-transformation: "to redeem […] the past and to recreate all 'it was' into a 'thus I willed it'—that alone should I call redemption" (Z 139). The taunting demon and his dusty, antiquarian hourglass, intimating the eternal return of the *Same*, finally releases its last morsel of dust; the creature's inquisitive grin curls ear to ear; the brass contraption flips anew—

---

[5] Heidegger, Martin. *Nietzsche*. Vols. I&II. Trans. David Farrell Krell (San Francisco: Harper, 1991), 14.

[6] Nietzsche consistently uses the word "thought" when referring to the eternal recurrence. Cf., Nehamas, Alexander. *Nietzsche: Life as Literature*. (Cambridge, MA: Harvard University Press, 1985), 150.

what will you say?[7] Nietzsche brings us here to consider something profound about ourselves. One's response, either denial or affirmation, is never grounded in a qualitative assessment of the world, as distinct from the person. What matters is *who* and not *what*. The individual will be the only barometer. *Prima facie*, the redemptive perspective is uniquely aesthetic. One who has achieved a yes-saying disposition toward affirmation has attained *aesthetic autonomy*—what Nietzsche refers to as a "singular taste," where one measures and assess the value of the past, in terms of the present, for himself, under his own Proustian-like rubric (*GS 232; A290*). By "giving style to one's character," through self-creation, *amor fati* is made possible (Ibid). This explanation is shared with Nehamas, but we part ways on just how far it can reach.

The propositional interpretation, as I understand it, is already a concern of the parable, as something to avoid, but which nonetheless, is easily overlooked on the journey toward a yes-saying affirmation. Here, the later metaphysical relapse, of which Heidegger speaks, can be clarified by appealing to certain relations inherent to the earlier works; specifically, in what is problematic to Nietzsche's notion of *self-creation* itself: i.e., the constant threat of *self-coronation*, as a critical trapping in any potential pursuit of aesthetic autonomy. The individual is compelled to conceive of himself apart from conventional tradition, yet cease from crowning himself *last*; of claiming to have found a *final vocabulary* (the mark of Western metaphysics), or supposing to have uncovered the *ultimate ground of reality* (Being). The celebration of the subluminal over the subliminal can plunge into self-defeat; an appraisal that pulls us back to Platonism. Somehow, personal asceticism must become anti-Sartrean, anti-Kantian, and refrain from fashioning an image for *all* of mankind; from proclaiming that the singular taste one creates for himself is best for all. The autonomous-self cannot become a static plateau

---

[7] Descartes' "evil genius" (*malin génie*) tempted philosophers to abandon their material bodies, and with the successive amputation of each limb came the inevitable dismemberment of human passion and finitude in general: a necessary sacrifice for the privileging of *res cogitans* over *res extensa*. Once the empirical world and the material body are obliterated, the remaining mental surplus (*cogito*) becomes the ultimate vehicle of genuine Knowledge. Nietzsche's "demon" performs the opposite function. It re-animates the importance of the body and our human situation, via abandoning the *modus operandi* of Western metaphysics, and opting for a perspectivist position that disregards the pursuit of absolute, Enlightenment-brand, capital-T Truth. Aesthetic self-creation changes the traditional narrative, rather than further engaging it, shifting the reigning philosophical focus away from the epistemology of the Platonic-Kantian canon. Cf., Gadberry, Andrea. *The Cupid and the Cogito: Cartesian Poetics*. (Chicago: Critical Inquiry. Spring 2017), Vol. 43.

without falling victim to the metaphysical urgency to surpass human finitude and contingency. Self-creation needs to remain laterally imminent (e.g., as opposed to the vertical apex of a parabola), one mode amongst a variety of potential modes, each devoid of hierarchy, but forever disclosing of infinite possibilities.

Aesthetic tastes and self-definitions are non-stable (mirrored in the shifting stylistic patterns of Nietzsche's own works) and should always remain amenable to revision. Just as we said earlier, the goal of affirmation is not its total fulfillment, as an *end*, but the perlocutionary effect that is its *means* (self-creation), is its *end* (as *striving toward* the yes-saying character of affirmation). Rorty attempts to overcome this trapping of self-coronation by way of a resolve between self-creation and liberal solidarity; a merging of both private autonomy and public morality.[8] Whether or not he does so adequately rests outside the scope of this paper. The point here is that Nietzsche fell into the very temptation his philosophy addressed. And there is ample evidence that he became aware of this fact while writing the later notebooks that comprise the *Nachlass*: for one, the decision in 1888 to not publish the text, *The Will to Power*, and two, in defacing his manuscripts with shopping lists—retitling one: "*zahnbürste.*" [9] And yet, Heidegger insists: "only an investigation of the posthumously published notes in Nietzsche's own hand will provide a clear picture" (Heidegger 15). Regardless (of the issue of authorial intent, which is not our concern), the exegesis I am arguing for rests on a specific mapping, whose inter-relations cannot be overlooked or negated without omitting some pertinent or necessary element constitutive of the overall sense of the eternal recurrence to begin with. Ultimately, I answer the belated controversy (parable or proposition?) by regarding the latter as an entailment of the former.[10] The

---

[8] See Rorty, Richard. *Contingency, Irony, and Solidarity*. Cambridge: Cambridge University Press, 1989.

[9] The word "toothbrush" is written over the text in blue ink. Viewable at the *Nietzsche Archiv*.

[10] The editor of the Cambridge text, Rüdiger Bittner, in *Writings from the Late Notebooks* (2003), makes explicit the controversy surrounding current and past interpretations of the unpublished manuscripts left to Nietzsche's literary estate: "Firstly, and most importantly, the evidence shows that Nietzsche abandoned the project 'The Will to Power" early in September 1888, so that publishing a book of this title under his name falsifies his intentions," and furthermore, even if we waive his objections, "it is in any case arbitrary to arrange this material, as the editors of *The Will to Power* did" (xii). The table of contents Nietzsche had envisaged for the book, which were outlined and detailed in the fragments, is also ignored by Elizabeth Forster-Nietzsche and Peter Gast in their initial assemblage. Over a quarter of the material was excluded even before the

eternal recurrence, as a literal rotary cosmology, is nothing more than what Zarathustra would disregard as—another "hurdy-gurdy song."

§II. The Moment of *Grand Inspiration*

The stage of our scrutiny, beset by the revelation of the demon, began with a winsome and seemingly incidental stroll through a forest in the Swiss Alps, paralleling Lake Silvaplana. It was here, on an August afternoon in 1881, that Nietzsche recalls the precise moment of *Grand Inspiration*; the eternal recurrence was conceived in an abrupt and ecstatic revelation "6,000 feet above man and time." [11] A universe of endless, non-linear, cyclical temporality is by no means a new concept. Critics are quick to cite myriad world historical examples from western philosophy to eastern religion: Indic myths, pre-Socratic philosophy, Pythagoreanism, Dionysianism, etc. Nietzsche's earliest publications confirm that he was not only familiar with these religions and philosophies, but that he possessed a profoundly rich and detailed insight into each of them. As early as 1862, for example, Nietzsche produced an essay titled *Fate and History*, which describes a cosmic clock and "perpetual circles of time" (Safranski 223). Avid readers will recall *The Birth of Tragedy* and other works, where tremendous praise is given to Dionysus; a god who dies and is perpetually reborn. With this in mind, Rüdiger Safranski (in 2002) formulates, what I will soon argue is, the most fundamental question regarding the interpretation of the eternal recurrence: "Why would a long-familiar idea be so rousing, and why now?" (225).

In a letter to Peter Gast dated "August 14th, 1881," following the Grand Inspiration, Nietzsche reports of lamenting "tears of joy" (229). Safranski answers, without hesitation—"Astonishing as it may seem to us, it was the allegedly arithmetic and physical evidence of this doctrine that overwhelmed him" (228). I disagree with both Heidegger and Safranski regarding the event that took place in Sils Maria. The correspondence to Peter Gast in 1881, that describes the "tears of joy," more than likely, does not pertain to an emotive response arising from a bout of scientific insight, as Safranksi reports. I am confident in insisting that Nietzsche did not weep in jubilation over having discovered new proofs, in contrast to his reading of Julius Robert Meyer's

---

editors implemented their own changes and innumerable omissions. Therefore, all of the concise evidence we have regarding his struggle to develop cosmological proofs for the eternal recurrence and the will to power could just as well have been published under the title—"Discarded Ideas."

[11] Nietzsche, Friedrich Wilhelm. *Ecce Homo*. Trans. Walter Arnold Kaufmann (New York: Vintage Books, 1967), 295.

conservation of energy, or Schopenhauer's tangent point of contact on the endless clock of time; Nietzsche wept because of the psycho-existential impact he envisioned for himself and his readers in imagining the sheer transformative power of the *thought* he experienced: e.g., a pragmatism of the highest yield; an idea so densely provocative that its disclosure would be commensurate to nothing less than total destruction or personal metamorphosis; he feels himself on the precipice of something unprecedented—no reader, hitherto, will close the book without being marked.

The cosmological view, Nehamas similarly maintains, obscures the psychological consequences of the *thought* and detracts from the larger emphasis placed on the relationship it has to the development of the self; to which I would add, also undermines the inaugural revelation itself. It is obvious, at least from the *Gay Science* and *Thus Spoke Zarathustra*, that the eternal recurrence has infinitely more to do with the individual, which consists in striving for the circumstances that might give birth to an eternal "yes!" in all things, while having significantly less to do with the notion of an infinite, celestial relay of all phenomena. This literary foundation is not a naïve and underdeveloped stage in the evolution of the *thought*, but the expression of its most consistent and coherent meaning. Consider the genealogy of the idea, as stated in *Ecce Homo*, where Nietzsche reports that the character of Zarathustra occurred in tandem with the eternal recurrence, as "the highest formula of affirmation" (*EH* 295). From its inception, then, what Heidegger calls its *poetic utterance*, should not be considered a deficiency on the path to some more highly esteemed formulae; its non-literalism is inherent to the jubilating, lightning-strike epiphany, of which Nietzsche laments. Nehamas finds the most ostensibly theoretical sections of *Thus Spoke Zarathustra* to be, on closer examination, mere literary methodologies for psychological application. He focuses on two sections almost exclusively devoted to explaining the eternal recurrence. In *On the Vision of the Riddle*, he asks whether the *thought* is elaborated merely to frighten the dwarf into fleeing Zarathustra's presence (Nehamas 149); this is, undoubtedly, not an allegorical stage used to convey the outline of a proof-scheme deduction; Nietzsche is, as I contend, making a larger suggestion regarding the natural *timidity of humankind*— an exposition of the claim I made earlier relating to his supposition that the demon is speaking exclusively to one kind of listener. Man's first instinct, when faced with the challenge of the *thought*, will be *flight*; if challenged further, as in the case of a demon stealing after you, inquisitively, "into your loneliest loneliness,"—*resentment*! Mankind is happy to piggy-back up the mountain, so long as the preacher offers a doctrine that appeases their inherent desires and immemorial appetites. The eternal recurrence is not an immediately appealing or easy prospect to digest. It does not *appeal* to man's self-interest outside of his will to overcome himself. The dwarf is frightened off! It is a reading of this kind that is crucial to Nietzsche's concerns, and should not be overlooked. We should be careful, e.g., when Nehamas (although he offers the most terrific assessments of the early period) accounts for the later propositions in the early work: "It is therefore the will to power that explains why the demon offers us only the very same life" (Nehamas 156). We do not want to augment the connection of the *thought* (whose sense resides in the parable) by way of a questionable metaphysics, at all, if it can be avoided.

§III. Nietzschean *Redemption* Abolishes Deleutzschean *Chance*

Nietzsche often discusses power and the feeling of power, but *the will to power*, as a metaphysics of *force* and *becoming* (i.e., the popular notion to which we've become familiar), "is only [found] in the late writings, particularly his [unpublished] notes" (Safranski 75). In utilizing the will to power as a vehicle of elucidation an inconsistency opens (which any interpretation of the early works will fall through if examined through the lens of the *Nachlass*). As a proposition, the eternal recurrence must be defended against a reduction to Platonic *Being*. Deleuze's arguments, like Heidegger, are working from the top-down, assessing the earlier thoughts with the later notes: "In the eternal return being ought to belong to becoming, but the being of becoming ought to belong to a single becoming-active" (Deleuze 179). We know, from the early writings, that *becoming*, as an expression of contingency and human value over *Truth*, is itself, coherent with his early perspectivism: "We have arranged for ourselves a world in which we can live—by positing bodies, lines, planes causes and effects, motion and rest, form and content; without these articles of faith nobody now could endure life, But this does not prove them. Life is no argument. The conditions of life might include error" (*GS* 177; *A121*). Just as dead metaphors diachronically evolve to assimilate themselves into a seamless, literal grammar, so too, our truths are a matter of social contingency.[12] But once we take the physics of the eternal recurrence to be a literal expression, we find ourselves constrained to solving how these perpetual cycles, as *a return of the Same*, avoid the obvious contradiction of *being* against Nietzsche's affirmation of *becoming*: "The eternal return is itself the Identical, the similar and the equal, but it presupposes nothing of itself in that of which it is said. It is said of that which

---

[12] See Nietzsche's *Truth and Lies in the Extra-Moral Sense*.

has no identity, no resemblance and no equality."[13] And the only way out of this problem is to posit some crafty metaphysical extension, as in the case of Deleuze, e.g., whom identifies the "return [as] the being of becoming, itself.[14]" Philosophers and critics thus feel the need to complete a coherent picture and connect the will to power, and its enigmatic "play of forces […] as a becoming that knows no satiety," to the eternal recurrence.[15] What is ultimately more misleading is the *dice-throw explanation* as a means of illustrating Nietzsche's picture of affirmation and *amor fati*. Two distinct moments arise: "when the dice are thrown" and "when they land and form a specific combination[16]." Affirmation, on this account, means both that one affirm all possible combinations in the throw, and the same with all possible results. Man is said to be a "bad player," whom counts on a large number of throws to attain what he wants (*NP* 25); a "good player," by contrast, affirms the "chance" of the throw and the "necessity" of its outcome: "the affirmation of chance makes possible an *amor fati*" (Bogue 29). In sum, we are charged with accepting the unknown possibility of chance while in turn affirming and accepting any variable outcome as a necessity. There's several problems with this picture. For the sake of brevity I'll name a few. Firstly, the identity issue of the return's Sameness that Deleuze attempts to ward off, because of the being-becoming dichotomy, is at the same time what is central to the moral of the parable. A *return of the Same* is necessary to the demon's challenge and even more important to Nietzsche's intended psycho-existential effect of giving the greatest weight to each moment. Without the virtual-literary enormity of this eternally repetitive hourglass of self-same cyclical identity, the psychological consequence on the reader is lost. The emphasis on "chance" undermines the perlocutionary-effect of the eternal recurrence, which is neither an addition, nor an arbitrary appendage to a greater whole, but is necessarily constitutive of its sense. Deleuze cannot successfully assimilate Mallarme's poetic scheme, because it fails to properly explain, and therefore nullifies, fundamental elements regarding *amor fati* and the eternal recurrence. Ironically, he seems to be offering a clearer treatment of Mallarme, *qua* Nietzsche, rather than Nietzsche *qua* Mallarme.[17] Zarathustrean redemption

---

[13] Deleuze, Gilles. *Difference & Repetition*. Trans. Paul Patton (New York: Columbia University Press), 241.

[14] Bogue, Ronald. *Deleuze and Guattari*. (London: Routledge, 1989), 29.

[15] Nietzsche, Friedrich Wilhelm. *The Will to Power*. Translated by Walter Arnold Kaufmann and R. J. Hollingdale (New York: Random House, 1967), 550.

[16] Deleuze, Gilles. *Nietzsche and Philosophy*. Trans Hugh Thomlinson (London: Bloomsbury, 2013), 24.

[17] See *NP*: *section 14. Nietzsche and Mallarme*. 30.

is a seizing of the game, opposite pedestrianism, of fortuitous unpredictability—and transforming it into a "thus I willed it so" (Z 139). This can be achieved through an individual creativity that alters the perspective of the past: "In this new way of life the past itself becomes new: 'The will is a creator'" (Nehamas 160). By extension, "chance," for Nietzsche, is to be owned by the self-affirming individual, to such an extent that arbitrary eventualities, outside of our affective deliberation, are no longer discernable from our willful autonomy. To approach *amor fati* is to feel that chance no longer exists, because we have not "accepted any possible outcome," but willed the specific combination that is the *present*.

By analogy, the *Übermensch* is presented as that hypothetical *Over-man* whom has, despite life's indifferent chaos, positively affirmed all of its negative aspects. The patent literary constitution of this character is noteworthy, insofar as Nietzsche does not intend its fictional evolution to be an attainable object for mankind; it has the effect of an ideal that remains perpetually ahead of us; it leaves an impression behind in its absence; that is all. The notion of accepting any and all random combinations of outcomes, i.e., via *chance*, is simply all-too-human. Framing the affirmation of the eternal recurrence in a dice-scheme humanizes and devolves its abstruse mystery, which should, on the contrary, exist at a distance from our average conceptuality; instead, Deleuze's picture levels-down the imaginary difficulty inherent to the perlocutionary significance of the *thought*. The difficulty of Nietzsche's redemption, which is constitutive of *amor fati*, is meaningful insofar as it relates to the reader's reactions—to such imposing and magnanimous notions—as *the return of the Same*. But the crux is *redemption*, not *chance*; its virtuality and not its reality. We are never meant to become the *Übermensch* as an actual end, as though *amor fati* could ever become an easy feat (e.g., a plateau man might arrive at in the Darwinian sense). The Over-man is always ahead of us and is never an attainable object. The pursuit of something beyond ourselves constitutes an endless struggle—to strive for ever greater fathoms of creativity, style, and character, in such a way as to make a hypothetical rendering of *amor fati* less of a distant imagining and more of a living intensity nearly in our grasp. Though this hourglass is doomed to constant inversion, the active pursuit of "giving style to one's character" unveils the whole of one's temporal world, in its bliss, banality, tedium, and horror, as infinitely redeemable through the prospect of achieving aesthetic autonomy through self-creation (*GS* 232; *A290*).

In *The Convalescent* Zarathustra awakes to find his animals gathered in suspense; after *seven days* he has finally returned from his redemptive slumber. The reader is quick to catch on to the religious connotation and so are the animals, which now seem to symbolize mankind and discipleship: "How well you know what had to be fulfilled in seven days […] have you already made a hurdy-gurdy song of this?" (Zarathustra 218). He questions their desire for cruelty and correlates it to their desire for transcendent knowledge and martyrdom; attending tragedies and "crucifixions [they have] so far felt best on earth," to which he further adds, "[man] invented hell for himself, behold, that was his heaven on earth" (Ibid). Zarathustra does not want to be man's accuser, nor the reason for man's masochistic delight. He sheds tears of despair, but not of Christian pleasure from pity, self-punishment, or the discovery of man as evil, but in the realization of how small dogmatic insights are—and that he must accept them—redeem them, if he is to affirm the eternal recurrence; accept that they are necessary in his surpassing them. *The Convalescent* is the ultimate chapter, in the narrative I am offering, to the eternal recurrence. Zarathustra's seven-day slumber, not only relates to the Christian notion of the creation of the earth, but as Carl Jung reminds us in his opus on archetypes and the collective unconscious, there are several Eastern, Indian aphorisms that claim it "takes seven reincarnations to reach perfection." [18] Upon Zarathustra's return to consciousness, he has completed the final constitutive element of his *amor fati*— the notion of *redemption*: his great affirmation demands that we must also *own*, as though we ourselves had willed, all that is past, undesirable, and lowly. He now becomes something of a *bodhisattva*, capable of perforating the unknown cycle under which we dance in eternally forgetful revolutions; whom uniquely possesses, as psycho-pomp of the *love of fate*, its path and hidden secrets; i.e., self-affirmation. He knows the way and can direct his disciples. But what he must share is something his animals had not anticipated; the path is not toward Truth; there will be no monuments or immemorial saints of worship erected in his name. He guards against the typical trappings of sublime revelation and torture ceremonies; there will be no official church built upon Zarathustra's epigrams, verses, or ideals. The animals now beg for him to leave his cave and sing outside, aware of his affinity for inventing songs. But Zarathustra calls them "buffoons and barrel organs" for taking something that was "invented for [himself]" and turning it into a "hurdy-gurdy song" (Z 220).

So too, the eternal recurrence, as a metaphysical-cosmological Truth— is just another "hurdy-gurdy" song. No matter how sound the argument or cunning the deduction—a metaphysical sense will seal its fate as one more Sunday ritual in a helix-chain of rituals (i.e., one more proposition in the history

---

[18] Jung, C. G., and R. F. C. Hull. *The Archetypes and the Collective Unconscious.* (New York: Pantheon Books, 1959), 36.

of metaphysics). Therefore, we should not conceive of Nietzsche's call to overcome man (*Thus Spoke Zarathustra*, published in1883) through affirmation by way of the Demon's challenge (*The Gay Science*, published in 1882), via some literal explanation of forces parasitic to the will to power (*Late Notebooks*, written in 1985-88; unpublished)—but rather, that we keep the notion of *affirmation* within the potential metamorphosis of the individual character in *self-creation*. We can then refocus our efforts on potential problematics of individuality and autonomy, such as the problem of *self-coronation*, that I've found most threatening to the pursuit of self-creation.

The formal analyses we have encountered over the last century yield flaws in Nietzsche's logic for a simple reason. If Nietzsche had intended, even partly, a systematic disquisition of the kind Heidegger holds him to, he would have elaborated, in greater detail, the most plausible reactions to the eternal recurrence—to begin with. But, as we have already stated, the literature details only two psychological consequences. Why would Nietzsche ignore, or fail to consider, the numerous possibilities of *indifference*, and, affirmations formed through the guise of that *indifference*? Nehamas acutely recognizes this ambiguity and summarizes the most popular arguments from indifference in response to the challenge. The first view he considers is Arthur Danto's, whom acknowledges only the cosmological theory, and therefore, responds solely to the "actual fact of recurrence" (Nehamas 152). Essentially, anything we might choose or decide upon is bound to return and leads to what it has always lead to unraveling. Since this temporal knowledge is hidden from view, Nikos Kazantzakis also agrees, we need not concern ourselves with ends or consequences: "Where are we going? [...] Don't ask!" (Ibid). Ivan Solls, on the other hand, responds not to the actuality of the eternal recurrence, but to its potentiality in affecting the way one might live. As is the case with Kazantzakis and Danto, Solls takes the suprahistorical aspect—or rather, our inability to understand it—to be of the utmost importance: "I cannot possibly anticipate now my experiences in future recurrences or remember then what I am going through now" (Ibid). Since we are fundamentally agnostic in relation to other recurrent modalities, he further argues that, "some psychological continuity of this sort is at least a necessary condition for my being concerned with my self's future, the possibility that I may live again in exactly the same way I have lived already should actually be a matter of complete indifference" (Ibid). This is an extremely persuasive insight that demands some consideration. To paraphrase Nehamas, either this is an oversight of Nietzsche's, or the fact that he failed to even touch on a *third alternative*—presumes something much more fundamental; namely, "that he does not consider the recurrence a cosmological theory in any way" (153). If we assimilate this conclusion in conjunction with our earlier deductions, i.e., that the reaction, as exclusively two-fold is motivated by hyperbole, a full-picture begins to emerge that suggests nothing but the complete identification of the eternal recurrence as articulated in the parable.

It was the *psycho-existential impact* that made such a resounding and inspiring impression on Nietzsche; that which brought about a chorus of jubilating tears. In response to Safranksi, this moment is *new* insofar as the notion of the eternal recurrence, from Eastern Indic myth to Schopenhauer, has now become fully internalized as parable: "For me—how should there be any outside-myself" (*Z* 217).

§IV. The Moment of *Grand Temptation*

What would such a life of eternal affirmation look like? Whom might we have to become, such that we might praise the image of the eternal hourglass of time? *Redemption* is a necessary condition for *amor fati*, but it is by no means a bi-conditional element in this formulation. Nietzschean redemption pivots on the ultimate personal achievement of self-creation, which precedes the redemptive judgment of self-affirmation, by "giving style to one's character" (*GS* Ibid). It is not merely a valuation to be made from anywhere, but from a specific plateau of creative autonomy, that confers a unique meaning and perceptual capacity upon the observer. It is with new eyes that one looks back and decides that all things, no matter how infinitesimally small or horrible, are necessary. Therefore, *amor fati*, as the apex of *self-affirmation*, first demands individual *self-creation*. Ironically, this must arise from "becoming who one is," as paraphrased by the subtitle of *Ecce Homo* and asserted by Zarathustra. However, the expression does not mean "'who one actually was all the time' but 'whom one turned oneself into in the course of creating the taste by which one ended up judging oneself'" (Rorty 99). In this sense, Nietzsche's notion of the self is similar to his regard for truth, i.e., that it is created rather than discovered. It seems apparent that to *become who we are* is to actualize a certain potential. Undoubtedly, this must emanate, someway or somehow, from our own momentum and not from traditional clichés or common moral platitudes.

This is the meaning of "giving style to one's character," and why Nietzsche tells us that it is "a great and rare art!" (*GS* Ibid). An aesthetic of self-hood is here achieved through an active gauging of one's "strengths and weaknesses" for the purpose of "fit[ting] them into an artistic plan until every one of them appears as art" (Ibid). At which point, even our weaknesses become a "delight of the eye" (Ibid). It now becomes clear that an inward revolution must take place in which all the personal elements of one's self integrate coalesce into something greater than the sum of its parts. The ugly or incidental past is bearable by means of its being a necessary component in a self-proclaimed immaculate whole. The "artistic plan" overrides whatever parts may be undesirable through their assemblage in a greater, unified purpose. But, again, what might this self-evolution look like? The question itself is nearly defeating of the overall moral theme that is being established. Only the individual, alone, can answer such questions through his endeavors and redescriptions. Although, theoretically, we might wish to demand some exposition of these claims, we cannot escape the arch of the message that rests in perspectival, individual interpretation. Throughout Zarathustra we are only given a negative theology— a list of condemning threats that amount to the assertion: "do not follow me!" Strong and domineering natures will find a new "taste" under a "law of their own" by which they judge their predecessors as well as their own histories (Ibid). The pitfall that concerns us, which conceives of the eternal recurrence as a proposition and renders Nietzsche a mere metaphysician amongst a history of metaphysicians, occurs specifically when *self-creation* becomes *self-coronation*: when, in the words of Richard Rorty, one forges a final vocabulary or lays claim to the most primordial description—or, the *last* description; i.e., the Truth of the cosmos, a transcendental signified, or ultimate ground of being. But Nietzsche's motivation for the sublime, unlike Kant or Sartre, is not epistemic but aesthetic. The purpose of his metaphysics is redemption.

In becoming who Nietzsche is, then, having reintroduced the eternal recurrence as the *greatest weight* in man's moral struggle with himself and his finitude, he also finds himself as the inheritor of a *greater weight*: the visionary carries the pain of proximity to his own imaginings. This fact leads *me* to the following thought: did there not come a moment, when Nietzsche's demon— not the one he created for his readership of *free-spirits*, but the conjuring itself— would be reclaimed from its shadowy moment of inception…to ask, and, what of you—speck of dust!?[19] Might it not be here, in this *second moment*, when Nietzsche must have asked himself the same question he had asked of us, that his temptation toward the sublime became actualized in assessing his own redemption? To pursue the will to power as a proposition is at the same time an attempt to surmount his philosophy in a singular autonomy; a towering universal schema. Is this not the ultimate justification to ground Nietzsche's *amor fati* and *yes-saying character*? That all roads, past, present, lead to this prophecy; his pain, suffering, depression, mania and ceaseless pursuit of

---

[19] I'm not the first to consider the possible self-referentiality of the demonic challenge. Cf., Lukacher, Ned. *Time Fetishes*. (London: Duke University Press, 1998), 140.

knowledge, ending in a sublime aesthetic totality. In one sense Heidegger is correct to assume that we need the posthumously published notes to comprehend a coherent meaning—surely, I agree. The notes, as material evidence of a lengthy personal struggle (*self-affirmation fallen to self-coronation*) that plagued Nietzsche during the latter portion of his life, emanating from the original site of the *thought* in Sils Maria. The temptation, then, would be to posit an underlying substratum of becoming: a will to power, to serve as the metaphysical underpinning of the master-slave morality, the rotary cosmology of the recurrence, the force affirmed by the *Übermensch*, etc. Does the *Nachlass* not reveal a struggle to complete, what he held in the highest regard, as a singular taste and in a definite "artistic plan" (*GS* Ibid)? We might consider a new reading of *The Will to Power* as a Proustian-philosophical project. Only, *Remembrance of Things Past* is a work of literary fiction, and thus does not risk (at least in the same sense) lapsing back into the history of Western metaphysics via self-coronation. Contingency, in the case of the novel, is affirmed through idiosyncratic eventualities and not philosophical sentiments. This may seem to be reaching; however, the influence that led Nietzsche back to metaphysics is not of the typical sort. He is not searching for the sublime in a Kantian or Platonic sense—for the sake of discovering or uncovering "reality." It is extremely unlikely that Plato had returned to haunt him, in the intellectual sense, especially after having spent his career surmounting the most provocative philosophy of perspectivism. Nietzsche's attempt at *self-coronation* does not arise from a desire to uncover the *actual* behind the *apparent* (a distinction he consistently held in disdain throughout his life), but to attain a singular position of aesthetic-autonomy that he would perceive as eternally redeemable. Thus, *The Will to Power* can be read as: *Assemblage of Ideas Past*.

"Mankind," for Nietzsche, is a means to greatness, a cultural "peak of rapture," in which all the horror and absurdities of the world become vindicated with the birth of genius: "there is no higher cultural proclivity" (Safranski 287). He outlines these thoughts in a later preface for *The Birth of Tragedy*, directly preluding the late idea of the will to power. Based on these dispositions it is hardly a matter of inference to assume that Nietzsche felt himself colossally constrained in his own redemptive assessment. Surely, the one whom pronounces, "I think I am too malicious to believe in myself" understands that there is only solace in perspectivism; his *becoming*, the never-ending flow that knows no end, is obviously not anchored in the belief of uncovering a final vocabulary or ultimate description of the *real* as opposed to the *apparent*. In 1888 Nietzsche declares: "I am no man—I am dynamite!" Forever critical of the dogmatism of philosophy and religion, he remains explicit: "there is nothing in me of a founder of a religion […] religions are the affairs of a rabble. I find it necessary to wash my hands after I have come into contact with religious people" (*EH* 326). It's possible that there is more to the matter of the will to power than the possible *Truth* it might portray as a systematic metaphysics. In recognizing the infinite play of unhindered forces, are we not ourselves prompted by an existential maxim to live in avoidance of immutable monuments, philosophies, ideas, and moral values? To be weary of all "otherworldly hopes" and "despisers of life" (*Z* 13); to always cleanse the intellectual pallet as one wipes away the beautiful lines and immaculate contours of a Chinese garden? The will to power, in its non-literal significance, summons the creative energies of humanity; it is the organic embodiment of the affirmative character that admits of no contentment or placidity, but forward striving, incessant aestheticism through re-description and re-creation. There is ever more to gain from a literary reading of the will to power: i.e., leaving its sense in its early Demonic-Zarathustrean poeticism.

§V. *The Will to Power*—Creative Reading

If there should be any appeal whatsoever to the notion of the will to power in discerning the sense of the eternal recurrence, it should be to further illuminate, ever more vivaciously and vividly, the rhetorical-allegorical stratagem of both concepts that were already existent in *Thus Spoke*. The reintroduction of the later (propositional) sense of the will to power can further solidify, through its own referential semiology, the world of the former doctrines. The elaborate structural play of the will to power can offer an underlying autonomy to the *Übermensch* and the eternal recurrence. The doctrines, themselves, yield profound significance even in the event that we detach any constraining notion of correspondence (de-metaphysis), i.e., truth, and conceive of each of them as non-literal figurations. On this view, any inquiry into the actual "reality" of these concepts seems to be beside the point. We should think of the Nietzschean doctrines just as we conceive of Deleuze's *rhizomes* or Sloterdjik's *sphereology*, where the meaning of their schemas is most evidently a matter of reshaping, creating, and extending frames of understanding through redescription, than an attempt to locate hidden, pre-existent structures.

What we have in-hand, regarding *The Will to Power*, as well as the later notes, published posthumously, is evidence of some flirtation with a pseudo-scientific metaphysics that contradicts an enormous body of prior work. We do not know the end he had in mind, except that he became dissatisfied with what he had found or created. In the absence of such qualification, we should opt for an exegesis that supplies us with a most *useful* and *logically consistent* narrative. I take

Nietzsche's pursuit of pseudo-scientism, or meta-pseudo-scientism, as a redemptive-aesthetic strategy to attain his *amor fati*. It is less likely that Nietzsche, in his later years, decided, after all, to join the transcendental search for knowledge, and more likely, that this event signified a moment of *Grand Temptation* (for self-coronation); to lay the foundational physics that would be the uniting principle of his major ideas; to become the Zarathustrian mouthpiece of a metaphysical ideal beyond all metaphysical ideals, which fundamentally, as we should insist, had more to do with a regard for himself, his own redemption (and, in turn, self-coronation); organizing his former philosophy by subsuming his ideas under a singular taste; gauging how he will view himself becomes a sublime pursuit (which has its own philosophical difficulties). If there is any metaphysical relapse it resides in the reductivism that is opened by the notion of aestheticism and autonomy. He is not looking for the absolute ground of anything, nor is he fighting the threat of falsity; his later work is a "prevention of the reduction to mediocrity" (*WP* 544; *A1053*). Regardless, most of the secondary literature we find ceaselessly pleads the contrary. What I suggest is entirely distinct from what is typical of Nietzschean commentaries: that we regard the triadic doctrine of the *Eternal Recurrence*, the *Übermensch*, and the *Will to Power*, as a unified allegorical stratagem, whose meaning must be discerned within the referential totality of its own elements and not validated or invalidated as an attempt for *Truth* that would seek to establish a correspondence outside itself. It is through the guise of this rhetorical medium that Nietzsche chooses to effectively communicate his most impassioned values and ideas. An alternate reading of *The Will to Power* and its relation to the eternal recurrence is not only possible, but textually consistent and historically coherent; only this time, the early sense will not be reconfigured, reframed, or swallowed into a belated or posthumous sense, but the exact opposite: one that recognizes its later metaphysical emergence as symptomatic of a possible blunder (the inverse of its own moral) introduced by the parable—the first utterance of the *thought* itself. The self-coronating, vertical point, must be stretched back to the horizontal plane of self-creation that affirms contingency, in its ever-emerging potentialities and possibilities for re-description and plural definition. Once we open this alternative reading to *The Will to Power*, as a Proustian-philosophical attempt, that, as an event, exploded from Sils Maria in a trajectory of self-creation—only to collapse under the antithesis of self-affirmation—we can focus on those issues inherent to self-creation that tacitly tempt us back to metaphysics from the outset. How we can achieve autonomy, *in the practice of philosophy in general*, without (self-coronating) esteeming a final vocabulary, or fashioning ourselves as the shamans of the *episteme*, of the *really* real beyond the apparent veil of Maya?[20]

§VI. Concluding Remarks

Amor fati—knows no limit—as the exclamatory response to the demonic challenge that forever alludes us, but ceaselessly tempts us to overcome ourselves. We encounter this Latin phrase, subtly and sporadically, always at random, in various nooks and corners: the fourth book of *The Gay Science*, in *Thus Spoke*, and *Ecce Homo*. Yet, it is the apotheosis of the hypothetical "Yes!" that parallels, in subtext, all of Nietzsche's writing since the afternoon of that winsome stroll. The yes-saying character of all things, as a romantic potential, remains a fervid presence. In "the fairest month of January," in homage to St. Januarius, Nietzsche grants himself a new year's wish: "I wish from myself today […] I want to learn more and more to see as beautiful what is necessary in things; then I shall be one of those who make things beautiful. *Amor fati*, let that be my love henceforth" (*GS* 223; *A276*). Man does not yet know how to sincerely and genuinely own this exclamation, and the demon, no matter how many sleepy homes he has crept in to, has yet to hear this utterance; but we are beginning to learn how a non-resenter might live. Zarathustra's teachings, parables, epigrams, etc., are exemplary of the beginning of that road, and to that end. Only, we will have to journey alone and discover for ourselves "how one becomes what one is," devoid of otherworldly comfort, proverbs inscribed in gold tablets, reassuring omni-daddys, or the warm guidance of a psycho-pomp: "Now, I bid you lose me and find yourselves; and only *when you have all denied me will I return to you*" (*EH* 220). We are on our own, armed with the memory and blunders of our predecessors, and the haunting challenge of the demon that ameliorates each and every one of our decisions, inflating the durational value of

---

[20] The twice-removed, meta-philosophical perspective of Derrida's *Postcard* might be exemplary: the first removal, a POV outside of metaphysics, and the second, outside the POV of the discipline in general…offering answers that combat the Plato-Kant tradition via continually shifting the narrative; if negation redirects us anew to the helix of history, then the best we can hope to achieve, as Rorty argues, is a Wittgensteinian therapy of those problems by perpetually replacing them with greater and more valuable redescriptions (e.g., as I responded to Deleuze on "chance" with an appeal to Nietzsche's "redemption"). On this Rortyian view, that fuses Nietzsche, Derrida, and Wittgenstein, a nominalist-bend is able to incorporate the praise of contingency without relapse or *self-coronation*. But too much seems lost; we feel left to Proust without the foresight of a genuine philosophical future. With this in mind, there is still much to be elaborated and explored in Rorty's *ironism* and the further potential for integrating our private autonomy with the realm of philosophical discourse.

our moments into fleeting intervals of eternity. The greater weight now becomes the decisiveness with which we respond to our creative spontaneity, when we're left to wonder, what ever-expanding and immeasurably vast universes might we give birth to in this grand, inward implosion, once *self-creation* presides over otherworldly temptation and man becomes resolutely untethered.

Works Cited

Bogue, Ronald. *Deleuze and Guattari*. London: Routledge, 1989.

Deleuze, Gilles. *Nietzsche and Philosophy*. Trans. by Hugh Tomlinson. London: Bloomsbury, 2013.

Deleuze, Gilles. *Difference & Repetition*. Trans. by Paul Patton. New York: Columbia University Press.

Gadberry, Andrea. *The Cupid and the Cogito: Cartesian Poetics*. Critical Inquiry. Spring 2017, Vol. 43.

Heidegger, Martin. *Nietzsche. Vol. I&II*. Trans. by David Farrell Krell. San Francisco: Harper, 1991.

Jung, C. G., and R. F. C. Hull. *The Archetypes and the Collective Unconscious*. New York: Pantheon Books, 1959.

Lukacher, Ned. *Time Fetishes*. London: Duke University Press, 1998.

Nehamas, Alexander. *Nietzsche, life as literature*. Cambridge, MA: Harvard University Press, 1985.

Nietzsche, Friedrich Wilhelm. *Ecce Homo*. Trans. by Walter Arnold. Kaufmann. New York: Vintage Books, 1967.

Nietzsche, Friedrich Wilhelm. *Thus spoke Zarathustra: a book for all and none*. Trans. by Walter Kaufmann New York: Modern Library, 1995.

Nietzsche, Friedrich Wilhelm. *The Gay Science: With a Prelude in Rhymes and an Appendix of Songs*. Trans. by Walter Kaufmann. New York: Vintage Books, 1974.

Nietzsche, Friedrich Wilhelm. *The Will to Power*. Trans. by Walter Arnold Kaufmann and R. J. Hollingdale. New York: Random House, 1967. First English Printing.

Nietzsche, Friedrich Wilhelm. *Writings From The Late Notebooks*. Edited by Rüdiger Bittner. Trans. by Kate Sturge. Cambridge, UK: Cambridge University Press, 2003.

Rorty, Richard. *Contingency, Irony, and Solidarity*. Cambridge: Cambridge University Press, 1989.

Safranski, Rüdiger. *Nietzsche: A Philosophical Biography*. New York: W.W. Norton, 2002

Creative Works

When the Mind Beckons Itself...

Alec Ontiveros

Five years ago to the day that I write this, I subsiding in my academic sojourn, fell upon a thought, one which I could not put down. It was summer then, and I was taking advantage of additional classes to move my mind forward through its understanding of itself. Eager to scour the depths and breadth of Anthropology to understand where and what it is that explains why we are explaining any *thing* at all, I sat back in each class an observer of those who chose to observe humans for the sake of academic competence (as some odd mix between a posthumanist and a transhumanist, bridged together by their internal contradictions).

And while, one night away from the classroom, sitting in my happiest of happiness, among friends, a thought perched upon my shoulder, nudging me towards a realization that was progressively being affirmed or reaffirmed in the actions of the moment happening before me. It was, as it is most commonly put, a feeling of déjà vu.

Telling me that this moment now as I lived it I have lived it, and that is all it spoke, nothing more, as I looked upon the room...as I sat there upon the floor not gnashing my teeth...but laughing...not cursing...cursing...cursing...what? ...there was no demon...there was no weight...there was nothing...how the world at once felt like something had been unhooked...like the motion that had existed prior had gone off the rails...everything eerily different...but completely the same...and I content in myself...not asking what had happened before other than what this moment truly is....what makes it this moment...what is purely this moment...this I wanted to know more than anything so that I could match it to my thought to check if such and such was true.

I must make this clear, this thought did not arrive to me on the wings of late nights reading into Nietzsche, I had never heard the words 'eternal' and 'return' spoken together at this point.

All I knew of déjà vu was what I had learned of it through pop culture or investigations into parapsychology when studying psychoanalysis became too tedious and slow for a proper breakthrough. And if anything was on my mind at that point it was an intense reading into sustainability in the Anthropocene and understanding McLuhan's statement that 'media is the message'.

Those were my classes and in my own time I was looking into meditation and ways to release myself from the monotony of my boring, young-adult mind—just the same as most students try to do outside of school. So when this thought came upon me I did not have recourse to label it, other than the moment present as it was, trying to understand what it meant, how it could be a thought at all, how I could find myself within the repetition, and if it was truly real.

And there it fell upon me, a sort of paradox...cast within the mirror vision of my mind I thought perchance I might have become untethered, unbound from time. For if I live such in the memory of a moment either past or future, how could I know within which I am...the past or the future?

For this I labeled the thought the soothsayer's paradox, and describe it as such: If one can truly enter into the vision of a future moment, inhabit a future version of their self to witness the reality that will have unfolded to them by that point, would they thus not exist fully immersed within that moment laden with the memory of the past that had come upon the present to that point, and thus how could they distinguish the memory of what had happened between the moment of their vision and the riddle that had come upon them? For how could they determine which is the memory of their self still within the past that had not yet come beyond the present to this future, and which is the memory of that future self that could explain every moment up until this point?

They would surely be cast into a void, their past self swallowed up and they no longer able to distinguish between what was memory of memory and what was the essence of their self looking through the porthole to see the future. And thus how could they ever return to that past, and even further how could they ever come to be in this future moment if they could never return to their past self, and thus even further than the furthest point, what would remain of their past self, what is giving life to the essence that makes them question the reality of their present moment, this future in which they feel both a sense of a past and future simultaneously?

Sure we could break this down into what is "really real" and say that such detachment of mind and body is not possible, that surely we would still feel the "really real" beneath the vision, and be able to take off our masks and return back into what we were when we began. That the soothsayer could never fully enter into a vision of the future, could never fully understand the riddle of the future. Yet these counterclaims are still rife in speculation, that is to say what and what cannot be done, for as I sat within the dwelling of my déjà vu, I was not concerned with counterclaims of whether or not it was possible....I was unsure if I had become unstuck from time and I did not know if I lived in the past or a future coming to be.

Precisely because this was not an instance but two independent events. A week later I inhabited the exact same space in seemingly the self-same way. That is, those thoughts and feelings which had come upon me the first time returned. I lived a déjà vu again, but could point to exactly when it had already occurred, this moment just a week earlier. The events that transpired, that which was said, done, shown, all the same as a week before, even down to the déjà vu itself, such as a glitch in the matrix, not just a feeling of remembering, I had seen both instances and could point them out. Yet, I was not as docile as I am in writing this, for I was consumed now within the horror, not gnashing teeth, still, but a complete loss of body, as mind cast off did not know from whence it had came, was I still this mind the week earlier which has seen this vision or am I the self that is answering this riddle. I felt as if I was oscillating between two present moments.

And so this soothsayer's paradox came upon me again, it asked me to answer itself, to say what had remained, and beneath the vision, within the riddle, was the narrative of my speculation, the form of my personal anxiety that looked out to understand the experience. I sat perched between a horizon and a horizon, which when I passed through the moment became at an instance as different as the night and the day.

This personal anxiety revolved around the 4th of July. The momentous day in which so much death is swept under the current of jubilation, in which so many accept the horrors of the world, these struggles that are burdened by others for the pride of vanity in looking out at a world that "belongs to them". And as such, living between the currents of a University blighting the Southside of Chicago I felt tension between where to be physically, and where to really be within myself for such a day.

Yet this anxiety was lived, focused on the real, this passing of the sun, and within my paradox I realized such that I was within the future of my two déjà vus, for surely thus I had worried about the 4th of July within the first moment and was reeling from its passing in the second. And so difference truly arrived to return me into the pace of my wanton, summer days. Although I had found a focus, and place to lay my feet and move forward from this dwelling, I was not sure I had fully understood the solution, nor was I comforted by this anxiety being the difference itself, for I did not know if I had just arrived to this junction and what truly had occurred was just newfound memory or if I had simply come upon this moment again, and again I will receive it.

You see...this feeling did not leave, it crept behind me in the shadows of the day, for the next couple of weeks this essence of searching would return, mostly arriving at night, as I unsure if the moment had returned or I was just exhausted from the day, or conversely I very sure that it had—a feeling that the day was just a memory and the night was all there truly was. Its consistency, or inconsistency, felt like a small plane sputtering for take-off. And in its tumultuous ascension I became unsure of which was the ground and which was the air, if I was instead landing rather than flying.

For now with this anxiety of its reemergence I became fully submerged in this feeling of déjà vu, it no longer left me, bringing questioning or taking it way, for both occurred at once. I was letting it occur, or so I told myself I was. As I did not focus on it, but let it live, as a silent passenger, and I the projection of its picture, looking out to the world to let it see what the world was, for it was through me this feeling lived, as it did not dance but on the comfort of my frame, for other's did not see it, it was not amongst their present moment, or whatever moment it was that they were living, I am not to say, but it was purely through my experience that it existed.

Psychoanalysis could take all sorts of form with this statement, use it as a testimony for the underpinnings of an insanity, at this point the sign of a departure from interacting with a phenomena for the lucrid attempt to live within the phenomenal, the characteristic venture into the void that signifies the need for outside commentary, a proverbial tether holding one to something as they venture into the abyss, and so I served that role for myself at the time. I was all there was to speak to about the return of my experience, for it is only I who experienced it.

Scouring through notes I had written prior to this point, I sought to see how it had been building, to understand the bent of this psychosis, as I read deep into Freud for a sense of meaning, a structure or recourse for my own treatment, and so I began to catalogue my emotions and my feelings, record what *it* was, and how *it* felt in the moment, hold memory for the memory of the present moment that had arrived.

And so the lingering fear of an entrance of insanity withheld itself as I felt a sense of control in *knowing* that it happened, accepting that *it* happened, and witnessing it *happen*, as if I was watching it watch reality through myself. This *it* that I was unsure of by virtue of it being so surely there...that *this* is the same, that the *way* that moved, or *what* they said or are saying, the light dancing on the wall, the image on the television, the importance of my day, my tasks, all held in the same gravity of a certain sameness, a crude but peculiar sameness.

And so this seeking to remember the remembering took hold of me, it caught wind of itself, and my déjà vu doubled, now this remembering the remembrance was remembered. I truly experiencing a déjà vu of déjà vu.

How the layer of self that had brought me through the soothsayer's paradox—that foothold of anxiety for the passing of phenomena, the horizon between moments, that which had been different, had been continuous—now was starting to be looked at by this *thing* within myself declaring the return of all things, this demon, or daemon that had come upon me to remind me of how my life is lived as I am living *it*. For in my quest to trap it, I surely trapped myself.

And how even further the beckoning of insanity had crept past my doorway to bring me out into the sun, bare and broken by the deceit of my own mind, or at least the racken calls of a world not like these thoughts within my head wanted me to believe, to conform to the currents of a present reality that did not fit within my own, that said that time's motion occurred once and a return was never possible. Yet my being detested such speech, for on this otherside all things wrung out a certain sound, leading me to discover why each thing was fixed to the moment within which it was in, yet these discoveries were written with words unspeakable, thoughts that only came out as noise. How now I stood between a doorway and the *otherside*, that place which gave grounding for these truths, and when I attempted to step back through the door its frame had vanished in the instant. As now mired in this otherside I was to remain. And so this outward embodiment of self I was able to still hold onto from before this all began, led me forward through my days as I but the shadow of its comport. I felt the weight of a world which would realize these words as the further pangs of an insanity, the schizoid mind bouncing amongst the pulls of paranoia, but it wasn't in anyway something built from absurdity that I became convicted in this feeling, and thus there was no confusion. The absurdity was simply that everything returned, there were no other lurking shadows explaining to me why, just myself cast beyond the vision of my self, there were no hallucinations of things which were not there, just the memory of what already is as it is itself, instead it was simply the same experience of being a person in the world, it is just that I remembered the way everything is the way *it is*.

Concern for Freud started to falter, for there was something more here than the criminal reproach towards my own neurosis, no longer could I cast witness to it as it unfolded as if I were a distant objectifier immune to my own speculation.

Instead, I sought towards the realms of the fringe, where the causal flips upon itself to suggest the motion beneath the incidental, some quasi-force which was apparently communicating something to me, or trying to make me aware of what was yet to come.

How I was gripped by a fear, castigating my limbs, wrenching my ankles as I felt swamped in the deluge of anxiety completely generated from within itself, a fear of death chasing after me to claim what I formerly was.

How felt the folly of my psychosis was, limited in its approach towards the world with this now faltering gaiety, it was but a spirit of gravity descending upon itself, a weight all its own that caused the forces of everything around it to fall towards *it*, and that rather than delight me, was the result of a repetitious beckoning of my own mortal coil—that around the corner of every instance perhaps was my death, and that this remembrance was because I had come to this stopping point so many times before.

And so I sought some type of bridge, between that which was apparent and the phenomenal aspects of my own inter-confusion—how could I have a déjà vu of a déjà vu, and what would be the significance of such a perspective. Within this searching for not that which I was seeking, but instead a justification for the seeking at all, of what it was that truly was *I* and what *I* is, I found myself looking into the archetypal structure of the Jungian universe.

I recall the moment which distinctively struck a chord within me: I, relegated to the refines of my own seclusion sat perched atop the street in my sunroom, with the light behind me as I sat watching a screen. Within this portal was an interview of Jung as he spoke about the likes of synchronicity, and how all of these thoughts he has come to form were not the result of some sort of dialectic—that is the constant overcoming of past confusions through the advancement of a superior logic; a searching for what is inferior and false in an effort to label what is true through diremption—but instead the motion of a thought which had preceded all of his becoming as a force which became that becoming. As if there was no distinction between the priorities of past or future action in the total formation of a moment, all motions dancing to the rhythm of the present moment.

The story goes that in his youth he was walking on his way to school when he was struck by a realization of his humanity, as simple as that. There was no prolific experience occurring before him ripe enough to awaken him to his mortal frame, but instead it was the repetition of his schoolyard days which shook him out of his mind to realize the difference the world had been living within beneath the frame of his self, and from that moment forth he ventured to bridge this perspective with that world outside, beneath, within—to ever expand his sense of wonder and purview so that he might capture the entirety

108

of the phenomenal within its grasp. And this grew into his ability to look forward into time with the same discerning lens he looked through into the past.

And here in this moment of deep reflection, as I sat pondering these words, with a synchronous nature that Jung would admire, a friend walked in the door to shake me from my seclusion within myself, and my déjà vu instantly tripled.

My sense of memory ejected from my being as I fell through the event horizon, as fear sat perched on one side casting my awareness of own mortality as it stretched the long path of time to become my understanding of where I had arrived. How this feeling of sameness stretched beyond the human projection we had collectively placed upon the earth, as beneath its guise the earth represented this sameness too. My mind torn from itself sought for a way back to being the being *being* it all. I read again into the science of parapsychology, an almost oxymoronic, but ironically not, concept, for in some sense it takes the same role as secondary criticism of philosophical text, it perfuse through streams of inquiry and intellect of other minds about other things, to find some semblance of meaning in the anarchy of the absurd.

From the piles of words I had scoured through only one tidbit brought itself forward as being relevant to the ensuing synchronicity: that light which passes through a crystal ball creates an effect within one's own perception of their vision that can cause the brain to overlay information that is not there except through that vision, and that this can occur when light passes through water under the right circumstances.

And there I sat upon the arm of a couch, watching a room of friends content in being the beings that they were, or at least outwardly it seemed, as I sat drenched in the vision of my déjà vu. The riddle had already quadrupled itself by this point, its redoubling too had occurred on the other side of this void I became consumed within, this *otherside* that remained within where memory had long since ventured. And within the light which had come to be directed from a lamp radiating its energy as it passed through water on a plate sitting before me, I beheld a new riddle within the vision. There sat a black-faced clock with green letters, digital numbers bespeaking to me 12:16.

How I admired the synchronous relationship with my reading and what happened before me, but also dismissed it as something I had created for myself, for I still held a thread attached to a thought which had remained outside of my mind this entire time: that maybe when this all passes I will just see it as something I had done to myself or my anxieties had done further to me, caused me to misperceive or to be unsure of what it was I perceived. I hoped that thought over anything else, but at the same time I felt also that this was the absurdity to believe in, not the absurdity itself, with the glaring sameness at every instance being so full and fulfilled with a newfound understanding of each thing as its thing-itself. My mind felt as a continuous stream of epiphanies to that point, I was not so much telling myself what the world was as it was telling it to me, my self a continuous unfolding out of itself.

A week later I sat within my childhood home among friends, different friends but friends all the same. I had travelled a great distance, and thought perchance with my travel I had outrun the déjà vu trailing behind. Yet it still tagged along, now tacked to my body like my shadow and my vision, pushing further yet away from the sense of what I was, as I now sat as the deflated self of that which was here before, the self that had lived in this space before this remembering had begun again, taking from me the sanctity of a self that was prior to this movement I was now drawing. As this recurring memory now took hold of even the deepest thoughts I might imagine within myself, no more was there any trace of whom I was without its ringing sound.

Unable to be this self any further I looked out to my friends, to my home, to all these aspects of my self that were no longer preserved, untouched by the quadruple déjà vus that I thought would soon leave me, and I felt my control of my own being dissipate like the sound of what was being spoken. My friends engaged in a conversation and my body listening, my mind discerning what it meant, while what I truly am sat so far away, deep inside my self, as a witness to what was unfolding. Each and every aspect of what it felt to be my self had returned as a form of the déjà vu, everything plagued with this realization.

Unsure of what else remained for this vision to purge, I sat upon the frame of my self and listened to the world happening before me. The television lied in the distance as my friends engaged in conversation with each of their selves. How I saw it before me, a show within a show, she the careful but prodding outsider to their contest between their selves. One such stood as Jung proving that he should have a place to speak for it is from his perspective that Freud gained a place at all, that is the wild and open unknown gave forth to everything. Yet still the other who resembled Freud in my mind spoke so absent-mindedly of the privilege that he held. To be able to say anything is certain at all is to hold your self above that which is said, and I watched as this Freud character of my mind tried to ignore this truth. As the two of them harassed her in their subtle ways, this she that stood as the object of their contestation, the affliction nature might surely hold, keeping itself from being perfect. And there I realized this privilege was all my own. To say that I was surely certain in all these things, these things repeating, this memory, this vision, this riddle, to say it was there, and say it boldly within myself, was now such a declaration, a loud and glaring call, of something within me that attempted to speak above it all, a dancing rhythm, a silent diction, giving way for the eternal conviction.

Once this aspect of my self, this final casting vision, the furthest from which I could be seen was revealed, pushed out into the light...it too began to return. How I felt my déjà vu had quintupled...yet when I sought to find the words to say this to another, that too had returned upon itself, for no longer was I outside of it anymore, but it began to become everything that could ever be, and thus in attempting to say sextuple was I met again by an unfolding of itself, and in seeking to remember what term came next I realized the door returned and had truly been opened, and on the other side was a mirror casting the reflection I had become.

My vision now having broken the outermost sphere, as the riddle coursed through each and everything declaring it had returned, it will return, it does return, it returns and yet too, I returned to it, to this returning returning within its return, to that mind that sat up within the chair, to the body that rested quite so still, for there was no longer a direction, but the infinite repetition already there to meet me, to meet my eyes and my gaze, as I lifted my head within that moment and looked upon the television to be greeted by the same bold-faced clock speaking to me 12:16.

Since that moment five years ago, this vision still sits beside me, finding its way into everything, as I seek to shape it, to turn it into something more than its glaring truth, to speak it as my own voice rather than let it speak for me—eternal return.

Book Reviews

Nietzsche and Transhumanism: Precursor or Enemy?—Edited by Yunus Tuncel
(Cambridge, UK: Cambridge Scholars Publishing, pp. 295, 2017. ISBN: 978-1-4438-7287-4)

Kevin LaGrandeur

With the burgeoning prominence of transhumanism over the past 20 years or so, a number of contentious philosophical discussions have erupted about how closely allied the transhumanist movement is with Nietzsche's philosophy. Some thinkers, including Max More (one of transhumanism's founders), claim that Nietzsche provides underpinnings to that line of thought, and that Nietzsche may even himself be called a proto-transhumanist. In *Nietzsche and Transhumanism: Precursor or Enemy?*, Dr. Yunus Tuncel bring together in one volume many of the most important essays that have appeared over the last decade regarding this debate. For the comprehensiveness and convenience alone, this volume would be worth reading; but an even more compelling reason to read it is that the essays it contains are vital to understanding the shape of this debate over the years. The book is arranged in three sections, comprising the three stages of the decade-long transhumanist debate: a set of essays that ran in *The Journal of Evolution and Technology* from 2009 to 2010; a continuance of that debate from *The Agonist* in 2011; and, finally, a third section that was written for this book. In what follows, I won't summarize each chapter; Dr. Tuncel does that admirably in the first chapter of the volume. Rather, I will dip into some major themes and arguments that this book contains.

First, in case readers of this review are more students of Nietzsche than of transhumanism, it may be useful to give a quick definition of that movement. In essence, transhumanists believe in purposely speeding the evolution of the human species by use of any and all scientific means available. These means include emerging technologies as well as more traditional ones, such as digital technology, pharmaceuticals, genetic engineering, and biotechnology. The ultimate aim of transhumanists is to create an advanced human species, one so advanced that it would be, in effect, another species of hominid: a posthuman one. Thus the terms transhuman (for humanity in transition) and posthuman (the completed project). This new posthuman species would be more robust, more mentally and physically powerful, and perhaps part machine and/or mixed species. With its biotechnical enhancements, this new humanity would have capabilities beyond humans of today, including longer lives; stronger limbs, bones, skin, organs, and senses; and increased brainpower.

Given this description, any reader of Nietzsche would see the possible similarity to his concept of the overhuman (*Übermensch*). And in fact, this concept has been one of the main subjects of debate throughout the years, as it still is in this book. Another Nietzschean concept most of the essays in this collection address is the notion of eternal recurrence, which some transhumanists see as a sort of exhortation for or anticipation of their project of promoting longevity and immortality in the human race. Those arguing for Nietzsche's ideas as proto-transhumanist also argue that his ideas champion science and technology over religion, a concept that also undergirds transhumanism.

In this book, the supporters of these kinds of parallels in the two thought systems are Stefan Sorgner—whose claim is that transhumanism and Nietzsche's philosophy have parallels; Max More—who says certain ideas in his seminal transhumanist essays stem from Nietzsche; and Paul S. Loeb. Although Loeb disagrees with Sorgner's and More's handling of the Nietzschean concepts of the eternal recurrence and of the overhuman (which he argues should be translated as "superhuman"), he agrees that those ideas are consistent with transhumanist concepts. For instance, he sees Nietzsche's concept of the overhuman as pertaining to future descendants as a group, rather than to one person of any time period (85).

Sorgner begins this philosophical donnybrook with an essay originally published in 2009 in *The Journal of Evolution and Technology*, and he is brave in facing mostly skeptical colleagues. He is relentless, as well. He has more essays in the collection than anyone else—four—and they are mostly dogged and diverse rebuttals that defend his notion that Nietzsche has had a strong impact on transhumanism (and indeed may be a proto-transhumanist). Nevertheless, his position is overrun by the many angles from which his opponents attack his premises. The most puissant points from his critics have to do with the nature of the overhuman, the eternal recurrence, and connections between them.

First, as Russell Blackford points out in his essay, the meaning of *Übermensch* is complicated; it has no exact English translation, being variously translated as superman, superhuman, overman, or overhuman (192). I like "beyond-human," but that is awkward–and the rest are not great either. But, in keeping with most in the book, I will use "overhuman."

114

In keeping with the contentiousness of defining *Übermensch*, two key objections mobilized against connecting Nietzsche to the transhuman claim 1) that Nietzsche's idea of the overhuman is centered on a self-overcoming in the sense of remaking one's inner self, not in supercharging physiological or mental abilities; and 2) that his idea of eternal recurrence is inseparable from the overhuman. According to the latter objection, eternal recurrence has little to do with the transhumanist ideal of physical immortality. Rather, it is posited by Nietzsche as more a test employed to discern whether or not one has attained an overhuman state, for a person in that state is the only one who has the inner fortitude to envision reliving his life without alteration of even one detail. Hibbard reinforces this idea when he raises the crucial point in his essay (196) that the overhuman and the idea of eternal recurrence are inextricably linked.

Most of the essays in this work continue to focus on the themes of the overhuman and eternal recurrence. These include intriguing essays by Sorgner, Michael Steinmann, and Russell Blackford (chapters 1, 10, and 11). Sorgner lays out the main points for the argument in favor of Nietzschian-transhumanist connections; Steinmann gives compelling arguments for why the overhuman doesn't really match the posthuman superman; and Blackford's chapter conveniently sums up the arguments to that point before taking a middle stance in the debate—that although Nietzsche may have some influence on transhumanism, the more pertinent precursors are Hobbes and Mill.

Indeed, as Blackford implies, most analyses of the transhumanist movement see its inspiration in Enlightenment philosophy, and many essayists in this volume agree with that. Several also agree with Blackford's point that Nietzsche's concept of the overhuman is vague. I am in this camp as well: after all, its main source is *Thus Spoke Zarathustra,* which is a long poem in which concepts are presented as aphorisms and metaphors, and so are open to widely differing interpretations. Michael Hauskeller (referencing Shapiro) neatly encapsulates this dilemma in chapter three: "Nietzsche has no clear concept of the overhuman and produces at best vague intimations of what he has in mind" (35). To complicate things, the concept of the overhuman may not refer only, or even mainly, to future humans. These intimations, as Hauskeller puts it, include *possible* examples of the overhuman in places where Nietzsche praises various historical figures for their possession of many qualities that match those of the overhuman. Steinmann, for example, notes a number of places where Nietzsche seems to list Goethe and Napoleon as examples of the overhuman (177). I would add to those sources Nietzsche's reference to Goethe again in *Will to Power:* "…one desires that faith should be the distinguishing mark of the great: but slackness, skepticism, 'immorality,' the right to throw off a faith, belong to greatness (Caesar, also Homer, Aristophanes, Leonardo, Goethe). One always suppresses the main thing, their 'freedom of will.'" (380, trans. Kaufmann). Those thinkers Nietzsche offers as examples here are all notable for particular common qualities: they think outside the box and do not play by the normal rules dictated by Christian or other foundationalist philosophies.

Sorgner, in his second essay—his response to section one—seems to see the genetic alteration transhumanists espouse as equivalent to the education Nietzsche valorizes as a road to the overhuman. But that simple insertion of change into individuals seems to undermine Nietzsche's idea of the work needed for personal change. In the case of the overhuman, striving (exercising one's will) is what leads to transformation (199).

After all this focus on the overhuman and eternal recurrence, Tuncel's chapter in part three of the book changes the focus of the debate, identifying transhumanist goals he finds incompatible with Nietzsche for other reasons. For instance, he brings up utopianism, which he argues is an essential part of transhumanist thought, and which he argues is out of line with Nietzsche's thought because it implies a dualism that is anathema to them. In particular, Tuncel claims, the idea that pain and pleasure can be decoupled runs counter to Nietzsche's ideas of the Dionysian and Apollonian: "Transhumanism is bereft of the Dionysian," says Tuncel, and so "life is ontologically separated from death, pleasure from pain." According to Tuncel, this is "endemic to a specific form of rationality that emerges in the Occidental world order," an Apollonian viewpoint that does not allow for the Dionysian and runs counter to Nietzsche (228). Moreover, "this is another aspect of ascetic idealism in the technological world" that diametrically contradicts Nietzsche's anti-ascetic philosophy (229).

In this section, Sorgner again gets the last essay, but he doesn't get the last word. Indeed, nobody involved in this debate settles for just stopping: everyone seems to want the last word here. This includes Sorgner, those who critique his and More's positions, Sorgner again, and then finally Tuncel, who has the advantage of being the editor and so perforce gets the last word on page twelve of the introductory chapter— the last chapter written before publication. All of this makes for a lively and amusing contest, roiling beneath its staid academic appearance with lively disagreement. The work feels less like a parlor discussion than a rollicking football game (American or European football, take your choice): despite the aim of good sportsmanship, the intensity of the game gives rise to the occasional sharp elbow being thrown until the whistle blows. In this case, even the referee – Tuncel – is a contestant, and can't resist taking the opportunity to close with a defense of his own position contra Sorgner and allies. This is clearly because Tuncel sees the debate as unfinished, his hope being that others such as "Steinmann and Woodward find a platform to respond to [Sorgner's] criticism" (12) in chapter fifteen— and because he clearly hopes that a future book in this series will be that platform. As he says in the last sentence of his introduction, "The debate shall continue." I, for one, sincerely hope so.

Works Cited

Tuncel, Yunus. *Nietzsche and Transhumanism: Precursor or Enemy?* Cambridge Scholars Publishing, 2017.

Nietzsche on his Balcony—Carlos Fuentes, tr. by E. Shaskan Bumas and Alejandro Branjer

(Victoria, TX: Dalkey Archive, pp. 332, 2016. ISBN 978-1-62897-158-3)

Nicholas Birns

A balcony is the perfect place for Nietzsche: not detached from life, but not in it either. Aware of the world, but also withheld from it. Not an ivory tower, not Olympus or Parnassus, but neither totally in the fray.

It would have been easy enough for Carlos Fuentes to write a book reflecting on Nietzsche, taking stock of Nietzsche's ideas. A novelist of his eminence could easily have found a publisher for that. In *Nietzsche on His Balcony, however,* Fuentes elects not only to go with his strengths as a writer, but to dramatize his engagement with Nietzsche. In this work, published a few years after Fuentes's death in 2012, Fuentes' authorial persona finds the man staying next to him at the Hotel Metropol is Nietzsche. Between balconies and across time, the two men have a coruscating – and, at times, moving – dialogue.

Unlike Marx or even Freud (as the recent work of Bruno Bosteels has shown), Nietzsche has historically had little impact in Latin America. Though currents of thought influenced by Nietzsche, such as existentialism, had a great impact on the region – and though Borges read him (along with, most likely, the polymathic José Carlos Mariátegui) – Nietzsche has been an under-articulated presence in Latin American cultural debates. Part of this lack of impact is the corrosive effect of vulgar Nietzscheanism. Fuentes has his Nietzsche say that "I was not anti-Semitic or fascist or nationalist" (330) and that his thought about "the will to power" was "distorted" by his sister Elisabeth. While this is quite true, in a Latin America whose cultural discourse leaned heavily left (and whose mixed-race majority meant that rhetorics of Aryan purism were unwelcome), the vulgarization of Nietzsche nonetheless tainted his reputation.

More recently, as Nietzsche's true complexity has been realized, writers such as Roberto Bolaño, Horacio Castellanos Moya, and Jorge Volpi have mentioned Nietzsche with more frequency. And indeed, though these younger writers are often differentiated from Fuentes in generational and ideological terms, Fuentes' late turn to Nietzsche in many ways heralds the greater attentiveness of the writers who came afterwards.

Fuentes depicts Nietzsche as a man of brilliant insight, but possessed of a fundamental estrangement from society, burdened with a sense of being misunderstood. It is this catapulting Nietzsche out of the social norm that enables Fuentes' Nietzsche to display curiosity about the novel's skeletal but intriguing cast of characters: the beautiful young woman Dorian, the socially concerned lawyer Aaron Azar, and the accused criminal Rayon Merci, who is Azar's client. These characters embody many of the issues that conventional views of Nietzsche see him as neglecting: gender, social injustice, and the workaday world. It is Fuentes' accomplishment to draw Nietzsche out precisely by having him interact with these invented characters in very different life-situations.

Nietzsche's first dialogue with Dorian, for instance, is about beauty. Dorian asks Nietzsche if Socrates, even though ugly on the outside, possessed inner beauty; she then quickly puts Nietzsche on the defensive by trying to get him to admit he was unfair to Socrates. Nietzsche does not budge— in reality, he never would, and neither would Dorian in her heart of hearts want him to. But Dorian does get Nietzsche to say mistakes are a way of bringing mystery to the world. True to form, Nietzsche casts himself as the anti-philosopher in this conversation: he tells Dorian, "I give you life, not reasons" (17). For this Nietzsche, however, life expresses itself in gnomic aphorisms, less in action than in insights which may or may not lead to action.

The Fuentes characters tell Nietzsche stories of various denizens of the world. Gala, for instance, tells the story of a Japanese student who walked into Carnival and killed someone in costume, not realizing it was a costume. Of this, Nietzsche remarks that "she could take care of herself" (46). Rather than acting as a salvific agent, Nietzsche here pounds a kind of nonjudgmental libertarianism. This is not a laissez-faire disregard of suffering, a manifestation of what Lauren Berlant calls "cruel optimism," but a detachment that shows compassion all the more by not presuming it can save the day. When Elisa, a sexually exploited girl, appeals to Nietzsche in the most plangent way, pleading with him as "Mr. Neachy" to save her, Nietzsche is clearly moved both by Elisa's plight and, perhaps, the sexuality evident in her appeal. In response, however, he points out that power manifests itself in either an absence of power or an abuse of power, and that if Elisa feels such an absence that is because someone else is abusing their power.

The stories are framed by Nietzsche appearing once a year, for a day, on the hotel balcony, as the societal changes and tales of injustice and suffering related in the first part of the book lead to open revolution in the second part. Fuentes illustrates how the abuses of the old regime lead to the excesses of revolutionary purity, as one of the new leaders, Saul Mendes-Renania, is a "pure ideologue" (304) who wanted permanent revolution. And just as Gala's female voice breaks through the quasi-authorial voice of Dante Loredano, so is Mendes-Renania's revolutionary zeal punctured by the more complex aspirations of his wife María-Aguila. Equally, Aaron Azar is a kind of *raisonneur* of the book, though there is a good deal going on in his world that his middle-level rationality just cannot process. As a kind of inverted Scheherazade—someone who listens to stories over a period of many years in punctuated annual reappearances, rather than telling a story continuously to keep themselves alive—Nietzsche is a surprisingly good listener, a fly on the wall who asks just the sort of curious and percipient questions an astute audience member of an experimental, long-form performance piece might ask. There is a fascinating tension between the literally embodied eternal return of Nietzsche—he comes back once a year, after all—and the evidence in the book that people change, history happens, people grow older and die, and even if the revolution does not change society, the people actually living in society feel its force as change.

The title is important to take note of here: in Spanish, it is "Federico en su balcón." The philosopher is called by his first name, and it is the Spanish Federico, not the German Friedrich. Even as the translators—who do a keen and supple job with this difficult text—keep the German and do not call him "Frederick," the familiarity and first-name basis are there as in the Spanish. It is not Nietzsche on *the* balcony, but Nietzsche on *his* balcony; Nietzsche speaks not from an authoritative Olympian perch, but from his perspective.

All this is rendered to the reader with a mixture of pathos and lightness— as a true *spoudaiogeloion* which places the book midway between treatise and popularization. Fuentes writes with rare tenderness not just of Nietzsche the philosopher, but of Nietzsche the human being: a man of "frugal foods" and "country walks," a man from the European North but drawn to the Mediterranean and the tropical, a man whose supreme insight is so perilously adjacent to his eventual madness. Fuentes' Nietzsche is both uncanny and benign, both a philosopher in dialogue with a supreme novelist and a deviser of his own impish and intricate supreme fictions. He is a "man of faith. Of a dangerous faith as it looks to the future" (342). Although this might not be the same future as the cathartic and mechanistic reversal of the power structure searched for by Latin American revolutionaries, it might, hints Fuentes, be a faith in a future so gossamer and preposterous that it actually might come true.

120

Works Cited

Fuentes, Carlos, et al. *Nietzsche on His Balcony: A Novel.* Dalkey Archive Press, 2016.

Being Wagner: The Triumph of the Will—
Simon Callow
(London: William Collins, pp. 232, 2017. ISBN: 978-0-00810-570-9)

Richard J. Elliott

While there are successes in Simon Callow's book *Being Wagner*, there are also significant failures. The most substantive success of the book is its accessibility. Written for a non-specialist audience by a non-specialist (Callow, while familiar with Wagner's musical output, is a relative newcomer to other aspects of Wagner's life), *Being Wagner* is an easygoing, readable book. Another success is that Callow's book is often genuinely funny: a hard feat for a biography treating a serious cultural figure such as Wagner. This is particularly so between pages 26 and 31, as seen in Callow's discussion of Wagner's wedding to his first wife:

> The heartless frivolity of the event chilled Wagner, he said. The pastor, at least, took it seriously – maybe rather too seriously, delivering a severe sermon in which he warned them of dark days ahead. There was, he said, a glimmer of hope: they would be helped by an unknown friend. Wagner perked up at this: who was this mysterious benefactor, he wanted to know. To his considerable disappointment, it turned out to be Jesus. (30)

Passages such as these certainly make for entertaining reading, but merits such as these are largely overshadowed by a number of failures of this text.

The first striking thing about this book is the, frankly, weird book cover: a famous satirical cartoon of Wagner, with an image of Callow himself protruding from Wagner's open cranium. One cannot help but infer a bit of arrogance, intentional or not, here. It is as if the author–or perhaps the publisher, hoping to shift more copies by placing the face of Callow, a successful actor, on the front cover–implies that this book will be able to do what other books on Wagner haven't been able to: to get inside Wagner's head. Although this is not the explicitly stated intent of the author, the cover gives one the sense that it just might be.

Both the title of the text and the author's rationale for writing it confirm these initial suspicions. Indeed, Callow hopes to discover "what it was like to *be* Wagner" (cover overleaf; italics mine)–or, as he remarks in the foreword, "what it was like to be near" him (xvi). The foreword closes with an orienting question for the text that Callow presumably intends to answer by book's end: "What was going on inside Wagner's head?" (xxii). Callow's reasons for providing such an account, one presumes, is that the author doesn't think previous biographies and works on Wagner have been successful in doing this; otherwise, why would Callow so heavily frame the book around this question?

In light of this orientation, one must ask: does Callow succeed in presenting what it was like to be Richard Wagner? In some places, arguably, yes; in many others, no. For a book that claims to offer insight into what it was like to *be* Wagner, it makes little attempt to clarify what is surely a central issue for providing such an insight: namely, what (and how) Wagner thought, and how his thinking developed. The lack of sustained treatment of the philosophical development of Wagner's thought–integral for successfully grasping Wagner's motivations for both the subject matter of his works, and his reasons for presenting them as such (and so, too, the often obsessively defined ways in which he dictated their performance)–is notable. When Callow does attempt to provide such a treatment, the end product comes out as weak or simply inaccurate.

One case of this is a particularly fascinating section voiced by Montmartre in *Death in Paris* that Callow quotes at length (44) yet leaves completely unanalyzed. In the section, Montmartre remarks:

> I believe in God, Mozart and Beethoven, likewise in their disciples and apostles; I believe in the Holy Ghost and in the truth of the one and indivisible Art; I believe this Art to be an emanation of God that dwells in the hearts of all enlightened men[...] I believe that all men are blessed through Art and that it is therefore permissible to die of hunger for its sake [...] On the other hand I believe that the souls of Art's true disciples will be transfigured in a shining heavenly fabric of glorious harmony and be united therein forever – may such a lot be mine! Amen! (44)

It is unfortunate that all Callow is able to muster about this truly telling statement is that it "may well have represented Wagner's deepest feelings" (Ibid.). Callow inverts the alchemist's trick here, and turns a passage that should be golden evidence for the kind of analysis he wishes to offer into something leaden, making this statement easy for the reader to pass over. A proper appraisal of this section would claim that it offers a telling insight into *what it was like to be* Wagner at the time of this writing. It utilizes satire and anti-religious lampoon to deliver a significant glimpse into the psychology of a man who holds the role of art integrally to the task of salvation. The failure to analyse such a significant passage calls the credibility of Callow's book into question. In this case, this is especially true, as *Death in Paris* remained one of Wagner's favorite stories, and he continued to return to it throughout his later life (reading it aloud to Cosima again in 1878, as we learn from her diaries).

This failure of Callow's, however, is best exemplified by his inadequate treatment of Schopenhauer's life-changing influence on Wagner. For instance, in his terse discussion of Wagner's "intellectual avenues" of pursuit (108), Callow gets Schopenhauer's philosophy flatly wrong when he writes that "Schopenhauer describes the world as an illusion, and an enslaving one at that, which can only be escaped by connecting to another dimension–that of erotic love" (109). He also writes: "the only human experience that is in any sense real [for Schopenhauer] is sexual love, which, in its all-consuming intensity, obliterates the material world" (ibid). He later describes "deep, transcendent, self-obliviating physical love, in the Schopenhauerian sense" (155).

The descriptions are short, yet this doesn't save them from disaster. Callow's descriptions here will be surprising to anyone who has taken the time to actually read Schopenhauer. (Somewhat incredibly, Callow at least at one point calls Schopenhauer's main work *The World as Will and Presentation* (111), which decent editorial scrutiny should have rectified.) Schopenhauer repeatedly offers descriptions of the sexual impulse as, variously, "the most decided affirmation of the will to live" (*WWR*, I, 328), something which Nature impels "with all her force" (Ibid., 330). In the second volume of the *World as Will and Representation*, Schopenhauer is consistent on these matters, arguing that the "[s]exual impulse is the kernel of the will-to-live and consequently the concentration of all willing" (*WWR*, II, 514), that it is the "invisible central point of all action and conduct" (*WWR*, II, 513), and that humans (or more specifically for Schopenhauer, men) are the sexual impulse made "concrete" (*WWR*, II, 514). Any distinction that might be exploited in support of Callow between sex and eros in a broader, less primal, and more intellectualized sense is rendered obsolete by Schopenhauer, who further writes of "that far-sighted, definite, and capricious selection for the satisfaction of the sexual impulse which is called love" (*WWR*, II, 536).

This theme continues elsewhere in Schopenhauer. In his *Essays and Aphorisms*, he writes, "Coitus is the sign that, despite every increase in illumination through the intellect, the will to live continues to exist in time"

(64/5). Not content with confining this description of the sexual impulse to metaphysics, Schopenhauer mixes in his notorious misogyny for good measure: "...has it not been noticed that sexual desire, especially when concentrated into infatuation through fixation on a particular woman, is the quintessence of this noble world's imposture, since it promises so excessively much and performs so miserably little?" (Ibid., 64) This stands in stark contrast to Callow's contention that Schopenhauer and Wagner were of one mind regarding recourse to the erotic as a form of salvation.

If Callow was unsure of his subject matter here, it would have been better to duck out of treating the intricacies of such philosophical exposition altogether, rather than offering the confused and inaccurate picture that he does. Although the "Acknowledgements" section at the end of *Being Wagner* has Callow thanking Bryan Magee for conversations on philosophical matters (221), it seems Callow could have benefited from a few more extensive conversations. Indeed, this issue is treated adequately in Magee's book, *The Philosophy of Schopenhauer*, which it would have been useful to consult (216–218).

Callow also fails to account for the development of Wagner's tensional and crucially insightful relationship with religion, and the prospects that one might glean from it any insights into what Wagner wanted–at least onstage–to promote: namely, a secular form of salvation. Like Wagner, Schopenhauer too had an uneasy relation with the notion of salvation (as the prospect of the "cessation of the will"). Furthermore, as in the case of Wagner, Schopenhauer's notion of salvation relies on religious rhetoric and experiences (drawn from Buddhism, Christianity, the *Upanishads*, and Plato) seemingly irreducible to purely secular or atheistic accounts. *Being Wagner* would have benefitted from a treatment of this sort, by discussing similar such issues in relation to Wagner.

Callow also leaves the development (or regress, depending on who you ask) in Wagner's religiosity insufficiently addressed. One might be reminded here of Nietzsche's proclaimed disgust at *Parsifal* as Wagner's "alliance of beauty and sickness," particularly given Nietzsche's idolization of Wagner during their near-decade long acquaintance. Nietzsche saw in Wagner a resignation in the face of what Nietzsche saw to be the life-denying tenets of Christian morality: given the grounds upon which Nietzsche offered this famous critique of Wagner, it would have been prudent for Callow to address the synthesis of religiosity and Schopenhauerianism in Wagner's later works. The issue of how and to what extent Wagner aligned himself with both a version of Schopenhauer's metaphysics, and to a particularly renunciatory version of Christianity, should have been covered so as to further promote what it was like to be Wagner during the production of *Parsifal*.

How this relationship between Christianity and Schopenhauerian pessimism bears upon the content of Wagner's ideals for his works, and the mind that wished to transmit this content (which Callow is aiming to get inside), is important yet overlooked. Although Callow draws attention to Parsifal's climbing the altar steps and taking the Grail–"Miracle of supreme salvation, the Redeemer redeemed!" (189)–he writes that *Parsifal* "is not a Christian piece. It is, at its absolute core, a Schopenhauerian piece: it rejects the world as nothing but a tragic illusion" (187). Such a claim seems to ignore the relationship between Christianity and Schopenhauer's thought, on a still-significant rhetorical level at the very least. Here, one ought to again think Nietzsche's analysis of Parsifal as a work that combines both a Christian ethic of renunciation and Christianity's unconditional will to truth. According to Nietzsche, however, such a combination reaches its culmination precisely in Schopenhauer's pessimism. Indeed, even Schopenhauer writes that "the true soul of the New Testament is undoubtedly the spirit of asceticism. This spirit of asceticism is precisely denial of the will to live... In this sense my doctrine could be called the true Christian philosophy, however paradoxical this may seem to those who refuse to penetrate to the heart of the matter but prefer its superficialities." (*Essays and Aphorisms* 62/3).

A final bone of contention: it is not at all clear what Callow is trying to achieve with the subtitle of the book, *The Triumph of the Will*. Is Callow trying to reclaim it from Riefenstahl's propagandistic usage? Given the controversies surrounding Wagner and his appropriation by the Nazis, this is a curious move, and one that is emblematic of Callow's conflicting claims regarding Wagner's relationship with nationalism. Thomas Carlyle once described the *Ring* cycle as the *Iliad* of the North: the *Iliad* bound the notion of ancient Greek nationhood around a mythical story, from which the Greeks took ideals about religion, conquest, social and political conduct, and the ethical life. So too would Wagner's Ring attempt to do this, as a created *Gesamtkunstwerk* intended to forge and demarcate a more concrete conception of German national identity.

At one point, Callow contends that Wagner was no musical nationalist (43), but this falls out of synch even with Callow's own descriptions both of Wagner and the *Ring* cycle. From the outset, Callow talks of the *Ring*'s "Teutonic tub-thumping" (xxi), describing its impetus as the promotion of a new "German" world based on pagan myths and heroic ancient figures (figures easy to "nationalize", as it were) (49, 89). For Callow, Wagner's Germanness underlies Wagner's artistic energies and creativity (48, 127). As a piece of evidence from Wagner's life that might evade the charge of offering (at least) an aestheticized form of nationalism, Callow discusses *The Ban on Love* and its Mediterranean influences (48–9); but aside from this early work and a smattering of other suggestive phrases, how convincing is the idea that Wagner embraced internationalist values, both in his life and in transmitting them into his other works? Indeed, Wagner's socialist tendencies were thoroughly nationalist; his critique of capitalism was firmly rooted in the *ursprünglich* German myths which he claimed resonated in the deepest chambers of his soul, alongside his quasi-Schopenhauerian outlook (104). Even at the relatively late period of the *Ring* and Bayreuth in his life, Wagner affirmed revolutionary tendencies, alongside his Christianity and a renewed commitment to his own form of German nationalism (177). Callow himself remarks upon this.

Thus in light of these conflicting passages, it is unclear what Callow actually thinks. It seems that Callow, while rightly willing to pass moral judgment about Wagner's anti-Semitism, is less willing to associate Wagner with nationalism. But the numerous examples from across Wagner's life–of nationalism, socialism and revolutionary politics–resonate together as one disturbing psychological disposition that Callow seems to ignore. Indeed, from the pseudo-history and the blood myths of the "The Wibelungs" essay of 1848 (143), to attempts to solicit the new Kaiser Wilhelm and Bismarck for funds (166), the evidence for Wagner's "musical nationalism" stacks up, even if Callow writes ambivalently about it. Of course, one need not be a musical nationalist (or indeed any other kind of nationalist) to enjoy Wagner. Given Callow's claims to be getting inside the head of Wagner, however, it is a shame that it is left unclear what exactly Callow thinks about one of the central issues of contention surrounding Wagner's legacy.

In sum, while Callow's *Being Wagner* serves as an accessible introduction to the life of this titanic and thoroughly Teutonic figure, it ultimately falls flat of its central aim and misunderstands key points of influence for Wagner. This biography offers only glimpses of Wagner's psychology, and given Callow's stated aims for the text, much more should reasonably be expected on this front. The book is replete with references to the un- or sub-conscious processes of mental life, both in Wagner and in humans in general (xv, 45 -6, 56, 57, 85 -86, 89, 147, 167, and 168), but rarely are such processes subject to the analysis they warrant. Any work that claims to provide an analysis of what it is to "be Wagner" really should be doing better.

Works Cited

Bryan Magee *The Philosophy of Schopenhauer, 1983* (2nd paperback edition; 1987). Oxford, Oxford University Press

Callow, Simon *Being Wagner: The Triumph of the Will*. London: William Collins, 2017.

Schopenhauer, Arthur *The World as Will and Representation in two volumes* (trans E.F.J. Payne), New York: Dover, 1969

---*Essays and Aphorisms*, Trans. R.J. Hollingdale, London: Penguin Classics, 2004

Nietzsche's Final Teaching—Michael Allen Gillespie

(Chicago: University of Chicago Press, pp. 248, 2017. ISBN: 978-0-22647-688-9)

Christopher England

Roughly half of *Nietzsche's Final Teaching* is composed of articles previously published between 1988 and 2009; the substantial new content extends the ideas therein and brings them together under a common theme. While it offers important insights on issues ranging from musicology to political theology, Gillespie's book is focused on the elucidation and critique of what he calls Nietzsche's "final teaching."

According to Gillespie, much contemporary scholarship – "particularly in the Anglo-American world" – privileges the more perspectival works of Nietzsche's middle period, thus failing to grasp the overall trajectory of his life and thought (17). By contrast, he argues that a truly radical inflection point in Nietzsche's project was reached in 1881 when he was struck by the idea of the eternal return of the same. This insight transformed Nietzsche from an ailing, little-known academic into the world-historical titan we study today (3). It also forced him to revise his prior thought (which he endeavored to re-present via the new prefaces of 1886) and develop a final teaching organized around the concepts of the eternal return, the *Übermensch*, and the will to power. This vision points toward both the nihilistic collapse of European civilization in a series of catastrophic wars and the reemergence of life-affirming values that could make a new beginning possible. Preparing the ground for this new beginning required not just the cultivation of a new existential sensibility, free from the spirit of revenge, but the creation of what Gillespie calls an "(anti-) metaphysics" that would replace the Western philosophic and religious tradition with a new vision of the whole, culminating in a political order that unpublished notes call "a thousand-year Dionysian *Reich*" (13, 20).

For Gillespie, the various aspects of Nietzsche's final teaching revolve around the meaning and practical consequences of the eternal return. He therefore situates his book as a corrective to post-war treatments that downplay the link between philosophy and radical politics in Nietzsche's thought (162).

Gillespie sees his reading as consonant with the more vexing Nietzsche we encounter in works by Heidegger, Klossowski, Leo Strauss, and Stanley Rosen (14, 213). And while he is careful to note that the works published after 1881 do not present Nietzsche's only teaching, Gillespie insists that contemporary thinkers, especially those who embrace liberal democracy, must come to grips with it, since Nietzsche's ideas "allow themselves to be used, but also make use of their users," shifting the commitments and sensibilities of readers in unpredictable ways (198).

The overall argument is organized around three main sections titled "Nihilism and the Superman," "Nietzsche as Teacher of the Eternal Recurrence," and "Nietzsche's Final Teaching in Context." The early chapters trace how problems associated with perspectivism gave rise to the concept of the eternal return. On Gillespie's account, the perspectivism of works like *Human, All Too Human* led Nietzsche into a labyrinth of despair in which he believed that "no perspective is truer or better than any other" and that all values could only be partial, since they must decay over time (77). Moreover, Nietzsche viewed this ethos as an historical fate that would soon beset all Europe in the form of nihilism. By contrast, the eternal return – a vision at once cosmological and existential – provides the resources for overcoming nihilism. In short, Nietzsche argues that because time is infinite but matter is finite, every aspect of the universe forms an interlocking whole that endlessly recurs (67). Each perspective, each way of life, is thus a necessary aspect of a universe that can only be accepted or rejected as a whole.

Gillespie argues that Nietzsche's attempt to envision a new cosmology of eternal recurrence is, at best, incomplete, largely because it remains entangled with what appear to be little more than assumptions about the nature of space and time. Indeed, he points to Nietzsche's lack of training in natural science as one reason why he was unable to produce even a working draft of the *magnum opus* he envisioned (21, 195). Nevertheless, as a kind of existential test, the notion of eternal return reorients Nietzsche's entire project because it points toward the *Übermensch* with the strength to overcome nihilism by affirming the whole, in all its horror and beauty. Such affirmation of the whole is beyond good and evil because it requires the active embrace of violence, mortality, and suffering as essential elements of life (55). Nietzsche, then, adopts a new role as the last disciple of Dionysus: he becomes the teacher of the eternal return whose work will soon provoke "the Great Noon," a moment of decision in which humanity will either choose to seek the *Übermensch* or collapse back into the hedonistic decadence exemplified by the figure of the "last man" (35).

The second section sidesteps these macroscopic issues and instead explores the myriad ways that the eternal return altered Nietzsche's writing. The chapter "What was I thinking? Nietzsche's New Prefaces of 1886" shows how he endeavored to re-present himself to public in order to prepare the ground for the final teaching. Before he could demonstrate what it meant to be the teacher of the eternal return, Nietzsche first had to indicate what he was *not*: namely, a Schopenhauerian pessimist, a Wagnerian romantic, a German nationalist, or an anti-Semite. Mostly propaedeutic, these prefaces offer glimpses of the final teaching in the form of a *via negativa*.

Perhaps the most original chapter in the book is "Nietzsche's Musical Politics." Here Gillespie persuasively shows that *Twilight of the Idols* is written in the form of a musical sonata, whose movements of thematic development and recapitulation are the closest that prose can come to displaying the process of eternal return. The sonata also represents a new "musical logic" in which the dissonant currents of European culture are harmonized in a new aesthetic synthesis (102).

The last segment of the book puts Nietzsche into conversation with two of his major interlocutors: Plato and Dostoevsky. In the chapter "Nietzsche and Dostoevsky on Nihilism and the Superhuman," Gillespie argues that whereas Dostoevsky embraces God's love to overcome modern nihilism, Nietzsche turns to a notion of power (158). Gillespie points out that this debate over the relative merits of love and power repeats traditional theological debates surrounding the central attributes of the Christian God: omni-benevolence and omnipotence. He thereby suggests that the final teaching retains unacknowledged links to the Christian tradition. In "Nietzsche and Plato on the Formation of a Warrior Aristocracy," Gillespie notes that the political thought of both thinkers centers on the uneasy relationship between eros and aristocracy. Aristocracy is a kind of political order that depends on a desire for higher things, but when left unguided, the   agonistic aspiration for what is noble can to lead to struggles over power and status that are immensely destructive. More specifically, both thinkers attempt mold and shape the passions of warrior class so that a viable political hierarchy can be sustained. Unlike Plato, however, Gillespie argues that Nietzsche is insufficiently attentive to the educational and institutional system needed to achieve this difficult task (175).

A running critique of Nietzsche's final teaching is scattered throughout the book. Gillespie observes that a good deal of middle ground exists between the simple alternative of the spineless last man and the heroic *Übermensch*. He also insists that European civilization was not as decadent as Nietzsche believed, in part because Christian morality and the secular trinity of democracy, rights, and equality have proven surprisingly resilient (xii). More interestingly, Gillespie attempts to show that even on his own terms, Nietzsche's later works "not only fail to come to grips with nihilism but exacerbate it" (28). On the one hand, Nietzsche's reading of Schopenhauer caused him to overestimate the prevalence of self-abnegation and passive nihilism in modern culture (37), turning him toward the radical assertion of human greatness. As Heidegger and others would later argue, however, it is hardly self-evident that this is the appropriate treatment for modern ailments (38). On the other hand, Gillespie argues that despite Nietzsche's attempt to move beyond Christian moral concepts, his thought remains firmly within the larger Christian orbit. On this reading, Nietzsche's vision of the eternal return depicts all things as linked under a common principle, an image that Gillespie calls "surprisingly monotheistic" (197). Furthermore, Nietzsche's understanding of will is unthinkable without the theological tradition that runs from Augustine to Luther (55, 186).

Some of what Gillespie has to say has been said before. Nevertheless, the significance of *Nietzsche's Final Teaching* lies with its sustained focus on the origin and meaning of Nietzsche's later thought, with its many scattered insights, and with Gillespie's lucid criticism of the project as it develops in the years following the publication of *Zarathustra*. Of course, much of what Gillespie writes about Nietzsche's intentions will be contested, but one need not agree with every aspect of his argument to profit from this excellent work.

Works Cited

Gillespie, Michael Allen. *Nietzsche's Final Teaching*. Chicago University Press, 2017.

Biographies of Contributors

Nicholas Birns is Associate Professor at New York University, USA, where he concentrates in general humanities, fiction in English from 1700 as well as literary theory. His books include *Understanding Anthony Powell* (2004), the co-edited *Companion To Australian Fiction since 1900* (2007). The latter was named a CHOICE Outstanding Academic Title for 2008. He is also the author of *Theory After Theory* (2010), *Willa Cather: Critical Insights* (2011), *Barbarian Memory: The Legacy of Early Medieval History in Early Modern Literature* (2013), *Contemporary Australian Literature: A World Not Yet Dead* (2015) and *Vargas Llosa and Latin American Politics* (2010, co-ed. Juan E. de Castro). He has published essays and reviews in The New York Times Book Review, the Australian Literary Review, the Australian Book Review, Arizona Quarterly, and Exemplaria; Studies in Romanticism, Symbiosis, College Literature, and European Romantic Review.

Richard J. Elliott is a School of Social Sciences, History and Philosophy (SSHP) Research Scholar at Birkbeck College, University of London. He has published work on Nietzsche, Heidegger, issues in moral psychology and the philosophy of psychoanalysis.

Chris England is Visiting Professor at the University of South Florida, where he teaches political theory and the history of political thought. His forthcoming article on the origins of modern liberal utopianism will appear in the journal *Theory and Event* in April 2018.

Rainer J. Hanshe is a writer. He is the author of two novels, *The Acolytes* (2010), *The Abdication* (2012), and a hybrid text created in collaboration with Federico Gori, *Shattering the Muses* (2017). His second novel, *The Abdication*, has been translated into Slovakian (2015), Italian (2016), and Turkish (2017). He is the editor of Richard Foreman's *Plays with Films* (2013) and Wordsworth's *Fragments* (2014), and the translator of Baudelaire's *My Heart Laid Bare & Other Texts* (2017) and Joseph Kessel's *Army of Shadows*. Hanshe has also written numerous essays on Nietzsche, principally concerning synesthesia, incubation, and agonism. He is the founder of *Contra Mundum Press* and *Hyperion: On the Future of Aesthetics*. Other work of his has appeared in *Sinn und Form*, *Jelenkor*, *Asymptote*, *Quarterly Conversation*, *Black Sun Lit*, and elsewhere. Hanshe is currently working on two novels, *Humanimality*, and *Now, Wonder*, and *In Praise of Dogs*, a photojournalism project with Valentina Camu.

Lawrence J. Hatab is Louis I. Jaffe Professor of Philosophy and Eminent Scholar Emeritus at Old Dominion University. He is the author of seven books and over fifty articles, mostly on Nietzsche, Heidegger, and ancient thought. His books include *A Nietzschean Defense of Democracy* (Open Court, 1995*), Nietzsche's Life Sentence* (Routledge, 2005), *Nietzsche's On the Genealogy of Morality* (Cambridge, 2008), and *Proto-Phenomenology and the Nature of Language* (Roman & Littlefield, 2017).

Dirk R. Johnson received his BA from Bowdoin College in 1985 and his Magister in political science, philosophy and German from the University of Bonn. He received his Ph.D. in German Studies from Indiana University in 2000. His monograph *Nietzsche's Anti-Darwinism* was published by Cambridge University Press in 2010 and his piece, "Zarathustra: Nietzsche's Rendezvous with Eternity," will appear in the forthcoming *New Cambridge Companion to Nietzsche*. His articles on Nietzsche, Darwin and Darwinism have appeared in numerous journals, including *Nietzsche Studien*, *Rivista di filosofia*, *Journal of Nietzsche Studies*, and *Tijdschrift voor filosofie*. He is currently working on a project detailing Nietzsche's relation to the sciences. Johnson is Elliott Professor of German at Hampden-Sydney College, Virginia.

Dr. Kevin LaGrandeur is Professor at the New York Institute of Technology (NYIT), where he specializes in technology and culture. He is also a Fellow of the Institute for Ethics and Emerging Technology, an international think tank, and a co-founder of the NY Posthuman Research Group and of the Visual Pathways Technology Consortium (for researching tech apps for the blind). Dr. LaGrandeur has written many articles and conference presentations on digital culture; transhumanism and posthumanism; Artificial Intelligence and ethics; and on literature and science. His publications have appeared in journals such as *CALIPSO: Online Journal of the Long Island Philosophical Society*, *Computers and the Humanities*, and *Science Fiction Studies*; in books such as *Eloquent Images: Word and Image in the Age of New Media and Beyond Artificial Intelligence: The Disappearing Human-Machine Divide*, which contains his essay, "Emotion, Artificial Intelligence, and Ethics." He has also published on Artificial Intelligence, society, and ethics in popular publications such as *USA Today* and *United Press International* (UPI). His book *Artificial Slaves* (Routledge, 2013), about the premodern cultural history of Artificial Intelligence and its foreshadowing of today's technology, was Awarded a 2014 Science Fiction and Technoculture Studies Prize. In April, 2017, his latest book, co-edited with James Hughes, was published. About the future of AI's displacement of human workers and how to meet this challenge, it is titled *Surviving the Machine Age: Intelligent Technology and the Transformation of Human Work.*

Jeffrey Lucas received his B.A. from UC Berkeley in philosophy (2011). His mentors were John Searle (Speech Act Theory), Hubert Dreyfus (Phenomenology) and George Lakoff (Metaphor Theory in Cognitive Linguistics). His Master's degree is in philosophy as well (CSULA). Currently, he is working with Dr. Jun Liu on a range of topics that include Derrida and Nietzsche. He has taught English and History at a myriad private schools in the greater Los Angeles area since 2011. He was born in Arcadia, California (1987); currently, he resides in San Dimas, California.

Alec Ontiveros is a Master's Student in Liberal Studies at the CUNY Graduate Center developing time philosophy and mediation theory. Through an experimentation in fiction, Alec created a mixed-media novel, titled *Trial of the Absurd* (2017), to explore how metaphor and narrative can create new perspectives for philosophical discourse.

Thaís Helena Smilgys is Ph.D. in Philosophy and General Theory of Law at the University of São Paulo, Brazil, with a research internship at the Universität Stuttgart, Germany. She is a member of the Internationale Nietzscheforschungsgruppe Stuttgart - INFG - Universität Stuttgart. She has published on Nietzsche, epistemology, logic, and philosophy of law.

Alessio Tommasoli is affiliated with Università Europea di Roma. His PhD is from in Università Europea di Roma, with dissertation "Cinesofia. A Practical Form of Cinema from Deleuze's Philosophy" (2016). He has taught at various universities: Professor in History of Modern Philosophy: Academic year 2016/2017 at Università Europea di Roma, course title "Grace, Freedom and Action from the Reformation to Leibniz, Descartes and Pascal"; Professor in the International Master of "Praktische Philosophie and Existential Antropology": academic years 2015/2016, 2016/2017, 2017/2018 at Ateneo Pontificio Regina Apostolorum – Università Europea di Roma. Practical Philosopher: private practice since 2015.

The Agonist-Fall 2018 Issue Call for Papers: Nietzsche on Fashion and Design

As an untimely thinker, one who often proclaimed the greatest task is to think against the grain, Nietzsche was not in fashion during his time. He is also not a philosopher often associated with the fields of fashion or design. Despite his notorious criticisms of "fashionable" ideas, an enthusiasm for elevating aesthetic values, and his interest in the body, he never mentions clothing. Furthermore, other than his brief discussion of "Doric architectonics" in *The Birth of Tragedy* and some offhand remarks from *Twilight of the Idols* ("The architect represents neither a Dionysian nor an Apollonian state…Architecture is a kind of eloquence of power in forms"), he rarely mentions architecture. Nietzsche is rarely mentioned in fashion studies, nor did he write to fashion magazines or theorize fashion (as Mallarmé, Simmel, Benjamin, Barthes or even Fink did). And while much has been written on the artists, dancers and composers that have found inspiration in Nietzsche's philosophical ideas, his influence on architects, urban planners and fashion designers— both directly (Karl Lagerfeld and Le Corbusier) and indirectly (Rem Koolhaas and Bruce Mau)—has been largely ignored.

As Nietzsche's fame has caught up with him posthumously, we are left with his philosophy, photographs of his austere, banal, and period-appropriate suits, and countless questions on his relationship to design. For the upcoming issue of *The Agonist*, we welcome contributions – from scholarly essays to artistic explorations – on what an engaged, critical dialogue with Nietzsche's philosophy from the perspective of fashion and design might look like. Possible topics include but are not limited to:

Fashion and philosophy
Design and philosophy
Nietzsche and architecture
What does/would Nietzschean fashion look like?
Fashion designers inspired by Nietzsche
The fashion designer as philosopher
Nietzsche and environmental aesthetics

To submit your work for review, please send an abstract of 250 words or a 250-word proposal of your suggested artwork to nceditors@nietzschecircle.com latest by **June 1, 2018.** The final paper submission and final work submission deadline is **August 1, 2018.** Please see the Submission Guidelines at http://agonist.nietzschecircle.com/wp/submission-policy.

Submission Guidelines

To be considered for publication in *The Agonist* we require:

- A page with your full name, your academic affiliation (if applicable), address, email, and phone number.
- A short summary (200-300 words) sent together with your work, indicating the topic of your submission.
- A 250-word bio, the length of your manuscript/submission, and a short list of prior publications.

Please use biographical listings of current contributors as models.

Essays should be between 3,000 and 5,000 words.

Contributors are expected to check all typographical issues, such as italicizing the titles of works of art, in the Word file. If there are issues regarding the appropriateness of the text, those matters will be discussed with the contributor. If there are proofing issues, the contributor will be notified to make the corrections. Submitted texts will not be altered by us. *The Agonist* does not return submitted manuscripts, accept unsolicited manuscripts, or consider manuscripts that are under review elsewhere or that have been previously published.

BOOK REVIEWS:
The Agonist accepts review copies of books on or related to Nietzsche (see About) and will seek reviewers to write on them. Book publishers interested in forwarding review copies can contact the editors at nceditors@nietzschecircle.com or you can use our contact form. Please submit initially a proposal for an essay, which must be original work by the submitting author. For further details, please see Submission Guidelines below.
Any work received that does not follow the appropriate guidelines will not be read. If you have any questions with regard to our guidelines or submission policy, please contact us

HOW TO SUBMIT:
The abstract (300 words maximum) and the submission should be sent to: nceditors@nietzschecircle.com. Once approved by the *The Agonist* Editorial Board, a deadline will be determined for the submission. The response time may vary from 2-5 weeks, so please be patient.

SPECIFIC GUIDELINES:

1. *The Agonist* uses the *MLA style* (see www.mla.org).

2. All submissions must be submitted as a double-spaced Word-document, using a point twelve TNR (12) font with 1" margins on all sides. For footnotes, please use point ten (10) font.

3. The paragraphs must be separated from each other; indent 5 spaces in the beginning of each paragraph.

4. Quotations that exceed three lines must be indented and separated from the body of the text into its own paragraph. The lengthy citations are also single-spaced, as are the footnotes.

5. Please note that page numbers go into the upper right hand corner with your last name.

6. Italics are to be used for author's *emphases*, book and journal titles, and foreign terms.

7. Quotations from Nietzsche's works should be followed in the main text by parenthetical references to the work in abbreviation followed by section or note numbers: e.g., (BT §7), (GS §124), (GM III §7), (TI "Ancients" §3). For a complete list of standard abbreviations, see below. The translation being cited should be indicated in a footnote to the first quotation from the work. If the author is rendering Nietzsche's German into English, each quotation should be footnoted with a reference to a standard critical German edition of Nietzsche's works, preferably the KSA. All other scholarly references should be given in the footnotes.

8. In the case of essays on visual art, images and captions should be embedded in the text. Images and caption texts must be submitted both separately (on a separate cover sheet) and as the Word file in order to be prepared for publication.

9. In the case of essays on visual art, it is necessary for the contributor to obtain images and caption texts. Generally, these are available from galleries and museum press or public relations offices, along with the needed permissions.

10. Images must be at least 300 dpi, at a print scale sufficient to fit properly in a normal-sized PDF file. (8 1/2 by 11 inches—please see current The Agonist PDF files for examples of the scale.)

11. *The Agonist* does not offer compensation to contributors.

12. Copyright for all published texts will be held jointly by the contributor and *The Agonist.*

13. Manuscript submissions and all related materials and other correspondence should be sent to: nceditors(at)nietzschecircle.com.

14. Books for review and all inquiries concerning books listed as received for review should be directed to the book editors.

STANDARD ABBREVIATIONS:

As noted above, references to Nietzsche's writings are to be included in the body of the essay using the standard English title abbreviations indicated below. With reference to translations, Roman numerals denote a standard subdivision within a single work in which the sections are not numbered consecutively (e.g., On the Genealogy of Morals), Arabic numerals denote the section number rather than the page number, and "P" denotes Nietzsche's Prefaces.

Unless the author is translating, the published translation used should be indicated with a footnote to the initial citation reference.
References to the editions by Giorgio Colli and Mazzino Montinari take the following forms:

Kritische Gesamtausgabe (KGW) (Berlin: de Gruyter, 1967—) is cited by division number (Roman), followed by volume number (Arabic), followed by the fragment number.
Kritische Studienausgabe (KSA) (Berlin: de Gruyter, 1980) is cited by volume number (Arabic) followed by the fragment number.

Briefwechsel: Kritische Gesamtausgabe (KGB) (Berlin: de Gruyter, 1975—) is cited by division number (Roman), followed by volume number (Arabic), followed by page number.

Sämtliche Briefe: Kritische Studienausgabe (KSB) (Berlin: de Gruyter, 1986) is cited by volume number (Arabic) followed by page number.

References to *Thus Spoke Zarathustra* list the part number and chapter title, e.g., (Z: 4 "On Science").
References to *Twilight of the Idols* and *Ecce Homo* list abbreviated chapter title and section number, e.g., (TI "Ancients" §3) or (EH "Books" BGE §2).

References to works in which sections are too long to be cited helpfully by section number should cite section number then page number, e.g., (SE §3, p. 142), with the translation/edition footnoted.

A = *The Antichrist*
AOM = *Assorted Opinions and Maxims*
BGE = *Beyond Good and Evil*
BT = *The Birth of Tragedy*
CW = *The Case of Wagner*
D = *Daybreak / Dawn*
DS = *David Strauss, the Writer and the Confessor*
EH = *Ecce Homo* ["Wise," "Clever," "Books," "Destiny"]
FEI = "On the Future of our Educational Institutions"
GM = *On the Genealogy of Morals*
GOA = *Nietzsches Werke* (Grossoktavausgabe)
GS = *The Gay Science / Joyful Wisdom*
HS = "Homer's Contest"
HCP = "Homer and Classical Philology"
HH = *Human, All Too Human*
HL = *On the Use and Disadvantage of History for Life*
KGB = *Briefwechsel: Kritische Gesamtausgabe*
KGW = *Kritische Gesamtausgabe*
KSA = *Kritische Studienausgabe*
KSB = *Sämtliche Briefe: Kritische Studienausgabe*
LR = "Lectures on Rhetoric"
MA = *Nietzsches Gesammelte Werke* (Musarionausgabe)
NCW = *Nietzsche contra Wagner*
PPP = *Pre-Platonic Philosophers*
PTA = *Philosophy in the Tragic Age of the Greeks*
RWB = *Richard Wagner in Bayreuth*
SE = *Schopenhauer as Educator*
TI = *Twilight of the Idols* ["Maxims," "Socrates," "Reason," "World," "Morality," "Errors," "Improvers," "Germans," "Skirmishes," "Ancients," "Hammer"] TL

= "On Truth and Lies in an Extra-moral Sense"
UM = *Untimely Meditations / Thoughts Out of Season*
WDB = *Werke in drei Bänden* (Ed. Karl Schlechta)
WP = *The Will to Power*
WPh = "We Philologists"
WS = *The Wanderer and his Shadow*
WLN = *Writings from the Late Notebooks*
Z = *Thus Spoke Zarathustra*